CHRISTIAN THEOLOGY SINCE 1600

By the same author:

AUTHORITY OF BIBLICAL REVELATION. 1946

TECHNOLOGY, COMMUNITY & CHURCH. 1961

DEUTERONOMY (TORCH BIBLE COMMENTARIES).
2nd ed., 1964

JEREMIAH (TORCH BIBLE COMMENTARIES).
2nd ed., 1966

CHRISTIAN THEOLOGY
SINCE 1600

by

HUBERT CUNLIFFE-JONES
Professor of Theology in the
University of Manchester

GERALD DUCKWORTH & CO. LTD.
3 Henrietta Street, London, W.C.2

First published in 1970 by
Gerald Duckworth & Company Limited,
3, Henrietta Street, London W.C.2,

© HUBERT CUNLIFFE-JONES 1970

SBN 7156 0520 8

Printed in Great Britain by Richard Clay (The Chaucer Press) Ltd,
Bungay, Suffolk

CONTENTS

INTRODUCTION

THIS book is a modest attempt towards establishing a trust-worthy perspective of the recent centuries that lie immediately behind us. The attempt is certainly dangerous, perhaps even foolhardy. But at the same time, it is absolutely necessary. We need such a perspective to help us to grapple with pressing contemporary problems. The best criticism it can receive is not any criticism of omissions or inclusions, any criticism of errors of fact or of judgment, but rather a better and more satisfying attempt to state what the true perspective is.

In what perspective should we see Christian Theology after 1600? What we see is an irreversible trend towards thinking that is free from ecclesiastical control. This think-ing faces its contemporary questions in the context of a historical perspective that covers every aspect of human life, a historical perspective that is sensitive to the ever-accelerated achievements of natural science. This trend is something that, in principle, the Christian can only thank God for, even though in detail there are unsatisfactory and unworthy features in it. But it raises difficult questions for Christian theology to which there is, as yet, no satisfactory solution.

Three things need to be said: 1—Christianity continues to be a live intellectual option, because the affirmation of Christian truth on the one hand, and an historico-scientific outlook on the other, are not, in principle, incompatible. 2—That being so, it is satisfactory to live by Christian faith, knowing that the problem of *how* Christian truth on the one hand and an historico-scientific outlook on the other are compatible is being continuously probed. It is a strain to live in a situation in which there is an unbridged gulf between

vi

faith and culture, but if that is the situation, it is satisfactory to accept it, because the alternative is worse. 3—It is not only true that the historico-scientific outlook poses questions to the Christian faith. The Christian faith also poses questions to those who find in the historico-scientific outlook a total intellectual grasp of life. It insists that there are intellectual treasures available to men which this method of itself cannot grasp, and that it is now, as earlier, more reasonable, more intellectually satisfying to believe Christian truth than to deny it.

The crucial question is, how do we apprehend this Christian truth? John Henry Newman in his University Sermon for 11th May 1831 explained the expression 'Wisdom is justified of her children' (Matt. 11:19) as follows: 'There is no act on God's part, no truth of religion to which a captious Reason may not find objections; and in truth the evidence and matter of Revelation are not addressed to the mere unstable Reason of man, nor can we hope for any certain or adequate reception with it. Divine Wisdom speaks, not to the world, but to her own children, or those who have been already under her teaching, but who, knowing her voice, understand her words, and are suitable judges of them. These justify her.'

Newman's words, after nearly a century and a half of investigation and discussion by the critical questing intellect of man, sound neither so offensive nor so stupid as they did to many in the nineteenth century. On the contrary, they show themselves to be far more perceptive than the unalloyed confidence in Reason to which many lent themselves. But though they contain a large measure of truth, they cannot be accepted just as they are.

For in the end the attempt to exclude the questing 'unconverted' human reason from the grasp of God's truth must fail. Unless human reason of itself finds something in Christianity which it can in all honesty and integrity affirm to be true, it cannot begin its work of apprehending what is there. (In so doing, human reason is not 'outside' the grace of God, for he sustains and blesses all his creatures, and the power of his redemption, though widely rejected, is a factor in the life of the world, whether men respond or not.) But having once begun, the mind in apprehending is transformed by that which it apprehends. The true judgment on Christian truth is not the judgment of someone who remains persistently outside what he is judging. It is the judgment of a mind who, always seeking the truth, has let the reality of the Gospel of Christ alter and enrich the very questions he asks.

The period after 1600 is not a period in which the characteristic nature of Christian truth is for the first time being exhibited and developed. That privilege belongs to earlier periods. It is rather a period of the emancipation of man. This is something that Christians must believe is part of the positive purpose of God, though its full gift to human life will not be seen till human autonomy and Christian truth are integrated. We are still in the situation in which we must ask 'What will man do with his autonomy? Will he accept Christian truth while rightly remaining emancipated?'

In this situation some elements in Christian teaching, which had been thought essential, are now seen to be not so. But it is even more true that in this age as in the preceding ones, Christians must bring the characteristic Christian conclusions to bear to change contemporary false or unsatisfactory conceptions. This is a perpetual process. The end is not yet.

I.—THE SEVENTEENTH CENTURY

CHRISTIAN THEOLOGY IN PROCESS OF TRANSITION TO THE MODERN WORLD

General Characteristics

Transitions to the modern world may be found in many places, for example in the disjunction yet close interweaving between faith and reason in the thought of St. Thomas Aquinas, or in the critical abandonment of the harmony between philosophy and theology in William Ockham, in the Renaissance or in the Enlightenment. But it is certain that in the seventeenth century there was a slow change in the general outlook of thinking people, which represents the watershed between medieval and modern.

In the century we find increasing dogmatic explicitness, narrow and restricted in outlook, and conflicting fiercely with competing dogmatisms. Protestantism and Catholicism had taken up their relatively permanent positions, and now wished to consolidate the ground they held. The way to do this, it seemed plain to all, was to make completely clear the only basis for truth. Neither toleration nor concession could be given to opposing convictions.

Yet this very spirit bred a resistance to itself. If truth is so completely certain, yet there are a number of truths all certain of themselves, ought not reasonable people to be a little cautious about where the truth really lies? The alternative to this is to heighten the clarity and dogmatic assurance of any one conviction of truth.

The process of conflicting dogmatism led inevitably to a separation between theology and religion to the hurt of both.

1

Theological truth demands not merely clarity but also a sensitive openness to the sources upon which theological conviction is nourished, and religion needs the critical and disciplining function of theology. But in the seventeenth century they tended to separate.

In addition, the great revolutionary force in the intellectual world was the slow growth of a temper of philosophy and theology influenced by experimental science. This involved a turning away from the symbolic thought of the medieval world, a questioning of abstract notions in order to find those securely grounded and the beginning of a philosophy finding its roots in human experience as natural science does. This meant an emphasis on the general aspects of Christian theology and the simplification of revealed theology. In such a philosophy and theology there is reliance in a new way upon reason, though to the Cambridge Platonists the part of the intellect must not be over-valued. It must be kept subordinate to the Spirit in man.

1. *Orthodoxy*

The Orthodox Church in the seventeenth century was the Church under Turkish rule. This had two consequences. On the one hand, the Church was on the defensive and sought primarily to maintain its position. In relation to other Christians this meant that it was on the defensive both against Protestants and against Catholics. But on the other hand, in order to do this, it had to use Western models, with the consequent danger of distorting the Orthodox position. The ablest Orthodox students under Turkish rule were sent to study in non-Orthodox countries in order to develop their thinking and to maintain a high standard of scholarship.

Both aspects can be seen at three points:

(*a*) In 1573 Lutheran scholars from Tübingen, led by Jakob Andreae and Martin Cursius, went to Constantinople and hoped to win the Orthodox to the teaching of the Reformation by presenting Jeremias II, the Patriarch of Constantinople,

with copies of the Augsburg Confession in Greek, together
with translations of sermons by Andreae. They asked for his
opinion on Lutheran teaching. The *Answers* of Jeremias
(dated 1576, 1579 and 1581) reaffirmed the traditional
Orthodox position on Scripture and Tradition, the sacraments, prayers for the dead and prayers to the saints. The
only things commended by Jeremias in the Augsburg Confession were its assent to the early Ecumenical Councils, and
its opinion on the marriage of priests.

(*b*) The relations of the Orthodox Church with Catholicism
were bedevilled by an attempt to bring about union in
Poland on the basis of the Orthodox Church submitting
to the authority of the Pope. In 1596 a Uniate Church
came into being, but it was repudiated by the continuing
Orthodox.

(*c*) It is the antipathy generated by the Catholic attempt
to dominate the Orthodox that accounts for the tragic career
of Cyril Lukaris (1572–1638) who became Patriarch of Constantinople in 1620. He was a greatly gifted man with a wide
interest in the whole of Christendom. To combat the teaching
and influence of Rome he used Calvinist theology, and his
Confession published at Geneva in 1629 asserted the superiority of the authority of the Scriptures to the authority of
the Church, excluded the Apocrypha, rejected the veneration
of ikons, denied the infallibility of the Church, asserted that
man is justified by faith not by works, accepted only two
sacraments and rejected the doctrines of transubstantiation
and purgatory. His death by strangulation was on a political
charge—he was accused of inciting the Cossacks against the
Turkish Government; but his theological teaching evoked
deep antipathy in the Orthodox Church. It was condemned
by six local councils between 1638 and 1691.

The most important of the Confessions that came out of
the attempt to repair the damage done by Cyril Lukaris and
to give a true account of Orthodox teaching was that by
Dositheus (1641–1707) which was ratified by the Council of

Jerusalem of 1672. In this we see the distinctive contribution which the controversies of the seventeenth century made in the theology of the Orthodox Church. The Orthodox were compelled to give more explicit teaching about the nature and authority of the Church.

In his Confession Dositheus safeguards the Orthodox position against both Catholics and Protestants. He repudiates both double predestination and the Pope as Head of the Church, and is liturgical rather than scholastic.

2. *Catholicism*

Catholicism in the seventeenth century was on the defensive, seeking to consolidate its position and outlook as against Protestantism. This it had worked out for itself in the Council of Trent (1545–63). Although this was a sixteenth-century achievement, it is the substance of Catholic theology in the seventeenth and eighteenth centuries. There were two main aspects of the Council—first, the reassessment and reaffirmation of the doctrine of the Church, and second, the reform of Church discipline. This second aspect had a notable effect in the resurgence of Catholic Church life in the seventeenth century.

The theology of the Council of Trent had three main emphases. First, everything depends on the grace of the Lord Jesus Christ, which is the controlling and all-important factor in the life of the Church, and it is insisted that in the life of the Church it is really present, and really transforms human life. This is made quite plain. On the other hand, the Council stressed the reality and importance of the response to and co-operation with this grace of the free-will of man which is diminished but not destroyed by sin. In the third place, it is insisted that the Church has the right to lay down the detailed conditions on which man can receive God's grace. This reception comes in a social and corporate way, and comes through the seven sacraments which in differing ways together cover the whole of life. In asserting this right of the Church, the utterances of the Council manifest a deep pastoral concern. At two points, however, this is defective. The theological ground for giving the bread only to the laity in the Eucharist is made clear, but no hint of any pastoral reason for doing so is given. And while it is said that the Council wants the laity to communicate at all Eucharists, the stress on the corporate character of the Eucharists at which the priest alone communicates, rather nullifies this formal contention.

The theology of the Council of Trent is a formidable statement of the corporate nature of the Christian life, and of the Christian's dependence on corporate human decisions and acts for the intimacy of his growth in grace. But it may well raise the question whether there is any legitimate appeal from the corporate life and decisions of the Church to the original sources of revelation, and to individual contact with God which may be life-giving, but in the short term is in conflict with what the Church has decided.

The doctrinal decrees contain four main sections:

(a) *Revelation and the Bases of Doctrine.* Here the Council received and venerated with an equal affection of piety and reverence the written Scriptures and the unwritten traditions. Of all the Latin editions of the Bible then in circulation, the Council held that the Vulgate edition should be considered authentic in public lectures, disputations, sermons and expositions. No one should presume to interpret Scripture contrary to the sense which the Church holds.

(b) *Original Sin.* The Council held that the entire Adam, through his sin, was changed for the worse in body and soul. Because Adam was defiled by the sin of disobedience, he transmitted to the whole human race not only death and the pains of the body but also sin which is the death of the soul. Only by the grace of our Lord Jesus Christ, which is conferred in Baptism, can the guilt of original sin be remitted. (In this Decree the Council noted that it was not including the blessed and immaculate Virgin Mary, the Mother of God, but did not develop the theme.)

(*c*) *Justification*. This is a complex and balanced statement, which needs to be understood in its own right, and with its own understanding of terms, and not simply as a rebuttal of Protestant teaching, which used some of the same terms with a different meaning.

The Catholic unease over the implications of Reformation teaching is specially to be seen in Canon XI: 'If any one says that men are justified, either solely by the imputation of the justice of Christ, or solely by the remission of sins, to the exclusion of the grace and the love which is poured forth in their hearts by the Holy Spirit and is inherent in them; or even that the grace by which we are justified is only the favour of God, let him be anathema.'

(*d*) *The Sacraments*. The Decree on the Sacraments begins by saying that through the Sacraments of the Church all true justice either begins, or being begun, is increased, or being lost is repaired. This statement is crucial for what follows. The Sacraments were all instituted by Jesus Christ our Lord, and are seven in number: Baptism, Confirmation, the Eucharist, Penance, Extreme Unction, Order and Marriage. They contain the grace which they signify and communicate it to those who do not put an obstacle in the way. Baptism, Confirmation and Order imprint on the soul an indelible character. In effecting sacraments ministers must at least have the intention of doing what the Church does.

Catholic theology in the seventeenth century is especially known for two versions of extreme Augustinianism: *Jansenism* and *Quietism*. Both stressed the omni-competence of God's grace, and the nothingness of man; but Jansenism combined this with a rigorous moral discipline, whereas Quietism held that the true believer had passed beyond the stage of sinning and so needed no discipline. The background to both is a debate about the relation between grace and free-will which goes back to the beginning of the sixteenth century, and another debate over the standards of moral conduct and the advice to be given to penitents, in which the Dominicans

and the Jesuits were in conflict both at the turn of the
century (1598–1607) and again in the middle (1656)—the
Dominicans taking the stricter, the Jesuits the more liberal
attitude.

Jansenism

Jansenism sprang from the posthumous publication in 1640
of a book by Cornelius Otto Jansen (1585–1638), Bishop of
Ypres from 1636. Its main theme is that all that is good in us
is the fruit of grace implanted in the individual heart by the
hand of God himself. Jansenism as a movement developed
mainly after Cornelius Jansen's death. It has three aspects:
1—The gift of grace and the limited scope of human free-will.
2—The moral demand of God for the discipline of human
life. 3—Jansenism as an ecclesiastical party within the life
of the Church.

The most famous name associated with that of Port Royal
and the Jansenists is that of Blaise Pascal (1623–62), mathe-
matician, religious genius and prose stylist. He became
known to the religious public from his eighteen *Provincial
Letters*, in which he attacked the Jesuit theology of grace
and the lax moral theology that in his judgment followed
from it, and in some instances, actually did. Notes for a
Christian Apologetic, the *Pensées*, were published eight years
after his death. They lay emphasis on man's greatness and
misery, the necessity of making a decision for and against
God, and the reasons of the heart. Pascal was no theologian,
and his sombre view of life and his uncritical Biblicalism
were against some of the fruitful tendencies of his own time.
But his searching aphorisms are a perpetual stimulus to
religious insight.

The ecclesiastical political aspect of Jansenism lasted a
long time. Five propositions extracted from Jansen's
Augustinus—the first two textually, the others by com-
pression—were condemned first by the Sorbonne in 1649,
and secondly by Innocent X in the Bull *Cum occasione* in
1653.

They were:

(*a*) Some commandments are impossible to just men.

(*b*) In the state of fallen nature no resistance is ever made to interior grace.

(*c*) For merit and demerit man does not need freedom from necessity, but only freedom from compulsion.

(*d*) The semi-Pelagians were heretical because they held that the human will could resist grace or accept it.

(*e*) It is semi-Pelagian to hold that Christ died for all men.

In order to try to save the Jansenist cause Antoine Arnauld was unwise enough to draw a distinction between 'right' and 'fact'. The Church had authority to condemn the propositions, but on the purely factual question whether they were in fact in the *Augustinus* it had no authority. Jansenists could say that they were not in the *Augustinus*; but no movement which has a passion for raising moral standards can shelter behind a technical quibble, to avoid unpleasant consequences. After this the moral authority of Jansenism was lost.

Quietism

Quietism is the term applied to the teaching of Miguel de Molinos (*c.* 1640–97), a Spanish spiritual director. His influence grew after the publication of his *Spiritual Guide* in 1675. He found the state of perfection in a complete transformation in God in which the will was completely annihilated. To this state all external observances and even moral endeavour were a hindrance. His teaching was condemned in 1687. The moral dangers in this 'soft' attitude towards human effort account for the hostility of the Church authorities to it.

Bossuet

Jacques Bénigne Bossuet (1627–1704), Bishop of Meaux, the great pulpit orator of the century, and one of the great masters of French prose, should be noted as expressing the

dogmatic certainty of the age. In his *Exposition of the
doctrine of the Catholic Church* (1671) Bishop Bossuet
expounded the Catholic doctrine on the positions repudiated
by Protestant theologians; and in his *History of the Variations
of the Protestant Churches* (1688) he gave an account of
Protestant theology from 1517 to his own time. He divided
Protestantism into two main bodies—the Lutheran, and that
including Zwingli and Calvin; but he also dealt with the
English Reformation from Henry VIII to Elizabeth, and the
history of the Albigenses, the Vaudois, the Wycliffites and
the Hussites. He showed up the variations in Protestant
doctrine and the conflicts they involved between different
groups against the background of the unchangeableness and
the unshakeable firmness of the Roman Catholic Church.

In his *Essay on Universal History* (1681) in answer both to
free thinkers and to Biblical critics he attempted to prove the
perpetuity of religion and the transience of empires. Biblical
criticism he dismissed as quibbles about numbers and names,
and free thinking as thinking that the universe was the result
of change. Providence rules the universe. It is to be seen not
only in the history of the Jews and of the Church, in the fulfilment of prophecies, but also in the rise and fall of states. The
Church itself is a perpetual miracle, and a striking miracle
of the immutability of God's purposes. In spite of his very
great gifts, Bossuet in his whole attitude needs to be seen as a
prophet of the past rather than as a creator of the future or
even as one who sensed in any way what it might be like.

3. *Lutheranism*

Seventeenth-century Lutheranism has behind it the
Augsburg Confession of 1530 which defined its position over
against Roman Catholicism, and the Formula of Concord
(1577) which found a solution to ultra-Lutheran disputes and
distinguished the Lutheran Church from the Reformed.

The *Augsburg Confession* is in two parts—the first doctrinal,
the second polemical. It teaches that men are justified freely
for Christ's sake through faith, when they believe that they

B

are received into God's favour. By Christ we have grace, righteousness and remission of sins. Men ought to do the good works commanded by God because it is God's will, and not through any confidence of meriting justification.

The ministry of teaching the Gospel and administering the Sacraments was instituted so that men might obtain faith. The Church is the assembly of believers in which the Gospel is rightly taught and the sacraments rightly administered. For the true unity of the Church it is not necessary that rights and ceremonies should be alike.

The Sacraments of the Word are effective in the Church even when they are delivered by evil men. The grace of God is offered in baptism, and children are to be baptized. The body and blood of Christ are truly present in the Lord's Supper and are there communicated to those that eat. Sacraments are ordained to be signs of the will of God and must be received in faith. Both elements in the Sacrament of the Lord's Supper are given to the laity because this is the command of the Lord.

Ecclesiastical power is commanded to preach the Gospel and administer the Sacraments. It must not be confused with civil power.

The *Formula of Concord* expressed the solution for the majority of Lutherans of the controversies which had arisen since the Augsburg Confession. It deals with Original Sin, Free Will, the righteousness of faith before God, Good Works, the Lord's Supper, the Person of Christ, Christ's descent into hell, Church customs commonly called 'indifferent' (*adiaphora*) and Predestination. On Predestination it says that neither God nor his election but men's own wickedness is to blame if they perish. It also deals with the necessary distinction between the Law and the Gospel. The Law is Christ's strange work, denouncing what is hostile to the divine will Christ's proper office is to declare the grace of God, to console and to verify. The Law was given to men for three purposes:

(1) that external discipline might be preserved, (2) that men

might be brought to acknowledge their sins and (3) that regenerate men might have a rule by which they ought to shape their life.

Once the basic theology of the Lutheran Church had been worked out, all that remained to do was to clarify in greater detail and greater precision what was involved. The men chiefly responsible for this were in the early period—Martin Chemnitz (1522–86) and Johann Gerhard (1582–1637); in the central period Abraham Calov (1612–86) and Johannes Andreas Quenstedt (1617–88); in the period of decline David Hollaz (1615–84) and J. W. Bauer (1647–1713).

Three emphases are dominant in Lutheranism:

(a) *On Purity of Doctrine*. With Luther it had meant primarily the authenticity of the Gospel as opposed to all distortions of it, but in the minds of his followers it became the purity of the one revealed theology which could be known, and made precise and safeguarded. This emphasis must be put first because it determined the way in which all questions were met. We ought to have sympathy with the Lutheran theologians in their attempts to translate the glowing religious insight of Luther in which so many facets were held together in an intuitive understanding into the cold prose of theological statement. Yet we must recognize that what was secondary to him they often made primary.

(b) *On Justification by Faith*. Here it is unfortunate that Luther's stress on what the grace of Christ alone can do for man should be expressed in these terms, which seem to put the emphasis on a particular human attitude. Yet the Lutheran theologians worked hard to make plain the fact that the grace of Christ was all-determinative, and the importance of good works as the outcome of a living faith, though having no place in bringing about salvation.

(c) *On the Unity of God and Man in Christ, with Far-reaching Exchange of Attributes*. The danger of this was that while it made clear that Christ was the divine Saviour it minimized his human reality. This Christological emphasis was the determining factor in the Lutheran doctrine of the Lord's Supper.

Five things may be said about the scholasticism of seventeenth-century Lutheran theology:

(a) The crucial fact, as with all scholasticisms, is that it did not keep in close enough touch with religious centralities or understand its important task in a humble enough way. The task of theology is to elucidate what is given in religious insight, in such a way that the clarification serves the religious insight which is determinative, and not vice versa. Related to this is the fact that there began to spread a new empirical way of thinking—first and determinatively in natural science, but spreading in the atmosphere created by scientific experiment into philosophy. To this new temper of thinking in their own time the Lutheran scholastics were either blind or resistant.

(b) The intellectual tool to hand was Aristotelian logic. This meant that great emphasis was laid on the concept of cause, and that the method used in dealing with reason and revelation was the same. As the content of revelation was limited to Scripture, this meant a narrower theological perspective than in that of Catholic scholasticism in the Middle Ages. The natural knowledge of God is not a saving knowledge, but because of it man is inexcusable before God. It is innate because the idea of God is by nature engraved on every man. By the use of reason in theology the existence of the true God as the source of supernatural revelation is proved. But in the use of reason the ideas of God, sin and faith were all depersonalized. In spite of the differences in outlook the transition from seventeenth-century scholasticism to the Enlightenment was one of considerable continuity.

(c) What the Lutheran scholastics concentrated upon was the once-for-all clarification of the authority of Scripture. (Here they hardened the trusting but critical attitude of Luther and many sixteenth-century Lutherans.)

(i) The Bible is seen as an absolutely infallible doctrinal authority, and its authority lies in itself. It is not something dependent on the inner witness of the Holy Spirit.

(ii) The Bible is literally the Word of God in all its parts. The human element is limited to men acting as amanuenses to the dictation by the Holy Spirit.

(iii) Not only is it the Bible as a whole, or the doctrinal truths in the Bible, which are from God. Every phrase, every word, every letter, even the vowel-points of the Hebrew Massoritic text, are determined by God's infallible authority.

(iv) The infallibility of the Bible does not only cover questions of religion and morals; it applies to history, geography, geology, astronomy and every other subject in the Bible.

(v) Every part of the Bible has the same authority as any other. The theologians looked in the Bible for proof-texts of Lutheran doctrine.

It should be noted that the motive behind all this is to establish the absolute certainty of the salvation given in Christ.

(*d*) A detailed *logical* discussion took place on the relation of this theology to the presence of the body and blood of Christ in the Lord's Supper. The heart of it was a discussion of the extent of the interchange of qualities (*communicatio idiomatum*). Are all the divine attributes communicated to the manhood? Is Christ's body everywhere or only in many places? Is its ubiquity absolute or dependent on the will?

(*e*) Lutheran scholasticism has suffered in later estimation both from the precise scope and rigid character of the theology expounded and from the nature of the methods. But it may yet have technical lessons for the construction of a different theology in other circumstances. The dogmaticians were good technicians, and some of their formulations and distinctions may be of service to later generations.

Reaction to Lutheran Scholasticism

Lutheran scholasticism produced a reaction from the religious intuition it had excluded. It is to be found in two forms, one vaguely Spiritualist, the other more linked with Lutheranism. The *Spiritualist* type has its roots in the thinking of Jacob Boehme (1575–1624). His teaching is a mixture of theology, philosophy, chemistry and astrology. The germ of all his thinking was given in his first book *Aurora* (1612). He has three main lines of thought:

(*a*) *A Trinitarian Understanding of God.* God the Father is the being of all beings. He is the ground of being. He is the abyss, the undefinable matter of the universe, neither good nor evil, but including the germs of both, unconscious and impenetrable. This abyss tends to know itself in the Son, who is light and wisdom, heart and mercy. It tends to expound itself in the Holy Spirit who is the gurgling, bubbling element in God; he is God in action.

(*b*) *Man and Sin.* In man in his present condition the imagination is the means by which the transcendent reality is known. Sin is false imagination.

(*c*) *Regeneration.* Unless Christ is born anew in man, church membership with all its obligations is absolutely useless.

The implications of Boehme's teaching were an emphasis on the inner allegorical word as distinct from the Bible, a free interpretation of trinitarian doctrine, emphasis on a thorough spiritual and ethical renewal of man as opposed to justification by faith, and on an eschatological outlook that looked towards the restoration of all.

The more churchly reaction, known as *Pietism*, had a growing influence through the work of Philip Jakob Spener (1635–1705). Spener's pietism was Biblical and Evangelical. In 1675 he published *Pia Desideria*—the programme of his reforming movement. After a survey of corrupt conditions existing in the Church, he made six proposals to reform them:

(*a*) An intensified study of the Bible. The aim of this to be a truer and richer personal devotion.

(*b*) A fuller use by the laity of their spiritual priesthood.

(*c*) Confession of Christ by actions culminating in love rather than an unsatisfying search after theological knowledge and prayerfulness.

(*d*) The exercise of charitableness in religious controversy, and instead of attempts to gain a controversial victory, sympathetic presentation of truth which tried to win the heart.

(*e*) The reorganization of theological studies at the universities to establish higher standards of religious life among both professors and students.

(*f*) The alteration of sermons so that instead of aiming to exhibit skill and rhetoric, they would aim to profit the hearer in life and death. These proposals were the outcome of practical experience. In 1670 the first private meeting for edification had met in Spener's home. Both men and women attended, seated separately from each other, and only the men were permitted to speak. The sermon of the previous Sunday was discussed, or passages were read from a devotional book. In later meetings passages from the Bible were the basis for devotional discussion.

Spener's independent attitude, as well as his attempt to give the laity a real part in church life aroused considerable opposition from Lutheran Orthodoxy, but in spite of that it won many eager supporters.

The heart of the Pietist movement which Spener led was its concern with *personal holiness*. Spener himself distinguished between a historical knowledge and a spiritual apprehension of divine truth. Because of this stress on personal holiness the pietists equated regeneration with conversion, and saw it as an inner change in man. This attitude was a stimulus to Christian activity not to be found in orthodox Lutheran circles.

But while Luther began with faith and saw the Christian life as its outcome, Spener put all his emphasis on piety as a sign of faith. Man is justified because by faith he practises love. This leads to Christian self-righteousness rather than the adoring love of Christ by the justified sinner. But it helped Spener to be the first Lutheran theologian to include theological errors among those covered by the forgiveness of sin.

4. *Calvinism*

Calvinism has no Confessional Statement to compare with the dominating authority of the Augsburg Confession, nor any theological analyses to compare with the controlling authority of the Formula of Concord. The unifying factor in Calvinism was the legacy of Calvin, and the variety in Calvinism is expressed in the multitude of Reformed Confessions.

In the seventeenth century Calvinism is in process of development, partly hardening itself in relation to alternative views, partly absorbing modifying thoughts into itself, and partly giving rise to new developments.

The canons of the *Synod of Dort* (1619) set out the Calvinist conviction of the absolute sovereignty of God:

All men lie under the curse of their sin in Adam, but God in his infinite mercy sent his Son into the world to save some. Some receive the gift of faith from God and others not, proceeds from God's eternal decree of election and reprobation. Election is absolute and unconditional and the non-elect are simply left to the just condemnation of their own sins.

The saving efficacy of the atoning death of Christ extends only to the elect, but intrinsically it is abundantly sufficient to expiate the sins of the whole world.

Man was originally formed after the image of God, with a true and saving knowledge of God, an upright will and a pure affection. But he revolted from God by instigation of the devil and, abusing the freedom of his own will, became blind in mind and obdurate in heart and will.

As a result all men are conceived in sin, and are by nature

children of wrath, incapable of any saving good, prone to evil, dead in sin and in bondage to it, and without the regenerating grace of the Holy Spirit they are neither able nor willing to return to God.

Yet it is not the fault of the Gospel if men refuse to be converted. The fault lies in themselves. But if they do respond, the response must be wholly ascribed to God.

God delivers the elect from the slavery of sin, but not wholly from the body of sin and from the infirmities of the flesh, as long as they live. On the other hand, God gives them a certainty of continuing true and living members of the Church and in the end they inherit eternal life. This certainty of perseverance is not a source of pride, but of humility, patience and rejoicing in God.

The *Westminster Confession* of 1647 affirms the same conviction of the absolute sovereignty of God modified by the conception of the covenants of works and grace. The Confession begins with the Bible and expounds its scope, inspiration, authority and sufficiency, as an infallible rule of faith and practice—the word of the Holy Spirit in Scripture being interpreted through the work of the Holy Spirit in our hearts. It expounds the Patristic doctrine of the Trinity and the Person of Christ (I, XVIII). It affirms that 'by the decree of God, for the manifestation of his glory, a fixed number of men and angels are predestined to eternal life, and others foreordained to eternal death'. But, it affirms, 'in all this God is not the Author of sin, nor is violence offered to the will of creatures' (III, V, IX, XVIII).

Chapters VI and VII set out a doctrine of the covenants of God with man. This doctrine was inaugurated by Johann Bullinger (1564–75) and by Caspar Olevianis (d. 1578) one of the authors of the Heidelberg Catechism of 1563, in a work on 'The Nature of God's Covenant of Mercy with the Elect'. The theory of Covenants, known as the 'Federal' Theology, spread widely in the seventeenth century, particularly through the work of Johann Koch (1603–69), commonly referred to as Cocceius. He distinguished a 'covenant of works' in the state of innocence, and a 'covenant of grace' after the fall—the latter in three phases: the patriarchal (before the law—Abraham), the legal (under the law—Moses) and the Christian (after the law—Christ). The Westminster Fathers more simply divided the covenant of grace, the offering of life and salvation by Jesus Christ, into two forms, under the law and under the Gospel.

No freedom of conscience is allowed in the Westminster Confession. Christian liberty is freedom from sin—opinions contrary to the Word of God are to be censured by the Church and dealt with by the power of the Civil Magistrate (**XX**).

The invisible Catholic Church consists of the whole number of the elect; the invisible Catholic Church consists of all those throughout the world who profess the true religion, and of their children. Baptism is ordained not only for the admission of anyone into the visible Church but also as a sign and seal of his ingrafting into Christ. The Lord's Supper is ordained for the spiritual nourishment of true believers and their growth in him. Worthy receivers receive and feed upon Christ crucified, and all the benefits of his death, but the substance of the bread and wine are not changed (**XXV–XXIX, XXXI**).

The Westminster Confession contains a doctrine of the Christian use of Sunday which is not to be found in any other European theology. God has appointed one day in seven for a Sabbath to be kept holy to him. From the resurrection of Christ, the day was changed to the first day of the week. It is to be continued to the end of the world as the Christian Sabbath. In it men are to observe a holy rest from worldly employments (**XXI**).

The civil magistrate must not assume to himself the administration of the Word and Sacraments or the power of the keys, but it is his duty to see that unity and peace are preserved in the church and that the truth of God is left pure (**XXIII**).

God has appointed a day in which he will judge the world in righteousness by Jesus Christ, for the manifestation of the glory of his mercy in the eternal salvation of the elect, who receive that fullness of joy and refreshing which shall come from the presence of the Lord; and of his justice, in the damnation of the wicked who are cast into eternal torments and are punished with everlasting destruction from the presence of the Lord and from the glory of his power (XXXII, XXXIII).

Modifications within Calvinism itself

The most interesting movement within seventeenth-century Calvinism is the *School of Saumur* in France, even if the result of its teaching was to harden Orthodox Calvinism and make it more rigid. The School had for its professors, after the year 1633, three men of great ability and learning. Each of them raised a special theme for Calvinist discussion. They were Moses Amyraut, the ablest of them, who pro-pounded a theory of hypothetical universal grace sub-stantially equivalent to a doctrine of universal atonement; Joshua la Place, for whom the attribution of hereditary depravity came before the attribution of the guilt of Adam's sin; and Louis Cappel, who taught that the text of the Bible is not rigidly uniform. None of this teaching destroyed essential Calvinism or made a great difference to it except in so far as any weakening at all in the affirmation of the absoluteness of the Godhead of God opened the way to a dissolution of the Calvinist conviction. The orthodox Calvinists published against them the *Helvetic Consensus Formula* (1675), composed by J. H. Heidegger (1633–98), reaffirming the theology of the Synod of Dort.

Representative theologians of orthodox Calvinism may be found in Johannes Wollebius (1586–1629) in the early part of the century; Gisbertus Voetius (1589–1676), who com-bined implacable polemics with a deep piety—he declared that purity of life and purity of doctrine imply one another; and François Turretin (1623–87), who in the explicitness and verbosity of his theological system represented a scholasticism about to be superseded. His son repudiated his rigidity.

Alterations of Calvinism

(a) *Arminianism.* Arminianism is the name both for a specific movement in Holland in the early seventeenth century, in which politics and theology were intermingled on both sides of the contending parties, and also for a wide anti-Calvinistic tendency which probably owes nothing at all to Jacob Arminius. At the beginning of the nineteenth century John Henry Newman treated the term as a blanket term covering many shades of disbelief of Christian truth. It is the specific movement which is discussed here.

The dispute between Calvinism and Arminianism cannot be solved by logic. It is a difference between two understandings of the Godhead of God. Calvinism holds to the absolute sovereignty of God, who rules over the universe and redeems men in such a way that the response of man contributes nothing to his own salvation. Arminianism on the contrary, believes that the nature of the Godhead is such that God weaves into his own redeeming action the free ethical response of man. Calvinism has the merit and defect of being absolutely definite; Arminianism the opposite merit and defect of indefiniteness.

Jacobus Arminius (Jacob Hermandzoon) (1560–1609) studied at Geneva under Theodore Beza, was elected minister at Amsterdam, and then professor at Leyden (1603). He was at first a strict Calvinist, but when he was asked to refute the teaching of Dirk Koornheert he became converted to the doctrine of universal grace and of the freedom of the will. He saw in the seventh chapter of Romans a legalistic conflict of the awakened but unregenerate man, whereas Augustine and the Reformers had interpreted it of the regenerate. After his death the leadership of the Arminians passed to Simon Bisschop (Episcopius) (1582–1644) and Janus Uytenbogaert. The Calvinists were the national and popular party and the majority of the ministers supported them. They accepted the

existing standards of doctrine, and stood for the independence
of the Church over against the State. The Arminians wanted
a change in standards of doctrine, and appealed to the State
against the Church.

The Arminians formulated their position in Five Articles
drawn up by Uytenbogaert, and presented them to the
representatives of Holland and West Friesland in 1610 under
the title *Remonstrance* from which they were known as
Remonstrants. It was these five articles of the Remonstrance
which were condemned by the Synod of Dort. The Remonstrance first repudiates five Calvinist convictions:

(i) Double predestination, before the fall and even before
the creation of man, without any regard to righteousness
or sin (the supralapsarian view).

(ii) God's ordination to save a part of mankind from the
consequences of the fall by his free grace, but to leave the
rest, without regard to age or moral condition to their
condemnation (the sublapsarian view).

(iii) That Christ died, not for all men but only for the
elect (limited atonement).

(iv) That the Holy Spirit works in the elect by irresistible
grace, so that they must be converted and be saved; while
the necessary grace is withheld from the rest (irresistible
grace).

(v) That those who have received this irresistible grace
can never totally and finally lose it (the perseverance of the
saints).

On the positive side, the Remonstrance affirms:

(i) Conditional Predestination. (God has decreed to save
those who by the grace of the Holy Spirit, believe in Jesus
Christ, and persevere to the end.)

(ii) Universal Atonement.

(iii) Man's utter need of God's grace.

(iv) But grace is resistible. (The Arminians insist that
their emphasis on conditional predestination and man's

power to resist divine grace does not in any way weaken man's utter dependence upon divine grace to think or do anything good.)

(v) The uncertainty of perseverance. (On this point the Arminians later went further and definitely taught the possibility of a final fall of believers from grace.)

It should be noted that though Arminians were condemned at the Synod of Dort, the triumph of their opponents was short-lived. Prince Maurice died in 1625, and his brother and successor, Frederick Henry, allowed the Arminians to return and establish churches and schools. Holland from then on became more and more a country of religious toleration.

(*b*) *The theology of Hugo Grotius.* Hugo Grotius (Huig van Groot) (1583–1645), the Dutch jurist and theologian, illustrates how the sharp outlines of Calvinist theology were blurred in the seventeenth century. He had Arminian tendencies, and was a friend of the Dutch statesman J. van Oldenbarnevelt.

Grotius' main theological work was *The Truth of the Christian Religion* (1625) in six books. His ultimate appeal was to the authority of the New Testament, but the enquiring mind must find and accept that authority. 'I am persuaded,' Grotius said, 'that truth is not otherway to be defended but by truth, and that such as the mind is fully satisfied with.' The authority of the New Testament Grotius found not in any certainty as to the authorship of the books but in the fact that the authors wrote what was true, because they knew the things they wrote about.

Grotius also invented a notable theory of the Atonement. Ostensibly it was a defence of the general Christian conviction against Socinianism, *The Defence of the Catholic Faith against Faustus Socinus* (1617). Christ, said Grotius, made satisfaction by accepting the punishment due to others. But why did God think it right to punish Christ? (1) As a proof of his hatred of sin; (2) that the law's authority might not be

endangered by the entire abrogation of punishment. This
theory of the Atonement as due to the Moral Governorship
of God, shifts the emphasis to an external factor without
meeting the acute criticisms of Faustus Socinus. But it is
symptomatic of the undermining of dogmatic systems in the
seventeenth century, which is as much a feature of it as their
being upheld in a rigid form.

5. *Socinianism*

Socinianism may be described as a rational Biblicism which
sprang from the Italian Humanist Movement. It is a
Protestant Movement, but one of a very different character
from that of the Classical Reformers. It did great service in
raising critical intellectual questions, and in pioneering in
social witness. But because it repudiated the doctrines of the
deity of Christ and of penal satisfaction, it has been regarded
with abhorrence by Catholic and Protestant alike, and the
assimilation of many of its critical questions and positions
has taken place without acknowledgment.

Its distinctive character was given to it by an Italian
religious teacher Faustus Socinus (1539–1604), who may
have been stimulated by his questioning uncle Laelius
Socinus (1525–62). The main works of Faustus Socinus are
his book on *The Authority of the Holy Scripture* (1570), in
which he sought to show that the history of Christ is con-
veyed in a record substantially correct, and which is the
pioneer work for later attempts to show that the Bible is
trustworthy; and his more famous work on *Jesus Christ the
Saviour* (1594), from which later thinkers drew arguments
against the doctrine of penal satisfaction.

The implications of Socinus' teaching were worked out in
The Racovian Catechism—published in Polish in 1605 at
Rakow, with versions in German (1608) and Latin (1609). The
final edition, published in Amsterdam in 1659, is the basis of
the standard English translation by Thomas Rees published
in London in 1818.

The Racovian Catechism is from the point of view of later

theology an odd mixture of naturalism and supernaturalism. It accepted the reality of God who has supreme dominion over all things, of the Virgin Birth and the miracles of Christ, the Resurrection, Christ's heavenly reign and second coming. It even thought that Christ ascended to heaven during his earthly life to learn the will of God, and came back to earth. At the same time, it was a radical criticism of some traditional doctrines. But from the point of view of the time it was a natural product when rational thinking within the assumption of the time is applied to the Bible interpreted without regard to tradition.

It insisted on the authenticity, sufficiency and perspicuity of the Holy Scriptures. It repudiated the doctrine of the Trinity and taught that God is one Person. Christ was truly a man (though conceived of the Holy Spirit, and born of a Virgin), but the Holy Spirit, which is an energy flowing from God to man, was indissolubly united with him.

It emphasized in a striking way the life of Christ culminating in his death as an example for human conduct. We are expressly commanded to imitate Christ in patience, in love towards others, in gentleness and humility—the virtues which shone in the whole of his life, and above all in his death.

It strongly opposed the idea that God forgives us because Christ by his suffering and death has rendered penal satisfaction for our sins. The idea that Christ suffered an equivalent punishment for our sins, and by the price of his obedience exactly compensated for our disobedience is repugnant to the Scriptures and to righteousness.

Nor did it accept the denial of free-will which the doctrine of predestination implies. It is confident that we have the power to obey God as he wishes, when we are strengthened by the divine aid and by a filial spirit. It is not rational to interpret the Scriptural testimonies in the sense of the false idea of predestination. For predestination would destroy religion by making it completely inevitable; and it would attribute to God injustice, hypocrisy and wickedness as the author of sin.

The importance of the Racovian Catechism for Christian theology is partly the particular criticism of traditional conceptions, which acted as a leaven in other positions, and partly the fact that this kind of radical criticism is henceforward a permanent part of the theological atmosphere.

6. *Quakerism*

Another of the catalytic forces in the seventeenth century, at least in England, is the Quaker Movement—the establishment and growth amidst intense persecution of the Religious Society of Friends who were organized as a distinctive Christian group in 1668.

This was founded by George Fox (1624–90), a self-taught genius, who lived the doctrine he taught, obeying the light of Christ, testifying to the power of God over all and steadfastly persisting in the love of God towards all who persecuted him. The Quaker Movement was ferociously persecuted in the first forty years of its existence. If we ask the reason for this, we find it in the fact that in a century when religion dominated men's minds, the Society of Friends contradicted important convictions of both Protestant and Catholic alike.

This can be seen in the one notable theologian of the movement, Robert Barclay (1648–90), who published his *Apology for the True Christian Religion, as the same is set forth and preached by the People called in scorn Quakers* in Latin in 1676 and in English in 1678. This is a commentary on fifteen theological theses which do not constitute a whole theological system but do bring out the revolutionary Quaker modifications of existing Christian theological systems.

Quakerism may be said to be a universal supernatural mysticism rooted in Christ. It is in no sense a confidence in the natural abilities of man, but a confident certainty that the Light and Power of Christ are as available to responsive mankind as the presence and power of sin, and that they are to be seen in the transformation of human life.

The main Quaker convictions which are so revolutionary are five. First the object of faith is, as it has always been, the

C

revelation of God by the Spirit. Scripture is a secondary rule
to the leading of the Spirit. Secondly, sinful man is subject
to the evil seed of Satan, and knows nothing of God until he
is united to the divine Light, but the Light of Christ is not
less universal than the seed of sin. Thirdly, Justification is
something which Christ brings about in us as he works in us.
Fourthly, Ministry and Worship are utterly dependent upon
the inward and immediate testimony of the Spirit—everything else, liturgical or extemporary, is will-worship and
hostile to God. The Sacraments are precious inner experiences
—the outward forms were used in the Church for a time, as
other practices of equal authority which have been dis-
continued, but the outward forms are only shadows of better
things. Fifthly, because God only is the Lord of the conscience, no one has any legal right to force the consciences of
others.

In all these there is an affront to entrenched theological
convictions—the appeal to the Inner Light as the primary
authority over against Scripture and still more over against
Tradition; the appeal to the power of Christ as available for
men beyond any knowledge of the Bible; the ascription of
Justification very clearly to Christ and not to human
achievement and yet its linking to the transformation of
human life which cuts across the Catholic–Protestant debate;
the turning away from outward forms of worship and
ministry which persist in their own right even though there
is no sensitivity to the leading of the Spirit; and the clear
testimony to freedom of conscience which broke decisively
with the main Catholic and Protestant tradition.

7. Philosophic Tendencies

The history of Christian theology can never afford to be
unaware of the context in which theology is affirmed; and it
is in a special way influenced, whether its relations with it are
intimate or distant, by philosophy. Seventeenth-century
philosophy exhibits continuity and change with the medieval
period. Where it is not consciously different, it maintains

much of the medieval approach and terminology. But there is a progressive emancipation of philosophy from theology in the century. And there is a gradual transition from Latin to vernacular languages as the natural instrument for philosophical reflection.

Five philosophers and one scientist are outstanding: René Descartes (1596–1650); Baruch Spinoza (1623–77); Gottfried Wilhelm Leibniz (1646–1716); Thomas Hobbes (1588–1690); John Locke (1632–1704); and Isaac Newton (1642–1727).

What the development of philosophy in the seventeenth century shows is the response of reflective thought to the growth and influence of natural science. This occurred in two forms, normally called *rationalism* and *empiricism*. They represent the response to two different aspects of the development of science. In the first place, it had become clear that nature could be understood by natural laws expressed in quantitative terms: to do this the application of mathematics, with the precise measurement it entailed, seemed a universal key. This involved, for philosophy, abstract argument, which seemed to provide the means of new knowledge about the natural world. On the other hand, the method of natural science was the method of observation and experiment. Knowledge about the external world would seem then to be built on sense perception and on reflection upon it. Confidence in abstract ideas not based on sense perception seemed very dubious.

This double tendency in an age of marked change, in an age when the doctrinal unity of Europe had disappeared, meant the slow decay of the medieval heritage of thought —though the confidence that the existence of God could be demonstrated by pure reason persisted through the century.

8. *Latitudinarianism*

The seventeenth century may be said to be a running fight between Calvinism and anti-Calvinism in England. At the beginning of the century the Church of England was strongly Calvinist. James I was strongly Calvinist and sent delegates to the Synod of Dort to support Calvinism against the Arminian Remonstrants. The change came late in his reign and in the reign of his son Charles I. The Commonwealth period naturally expressed a swing-back to Calvinism and the Restoration a new revolt against it. The situation is complex inasmuch as the main Anglican ground for opposing Calvinism sprang from an emphasis on the patristic teaching on Christology and the sacraments in the context of a new contention for the divine right of episcopacy. Within the framework of these strong dogmatic convictions, a wide freedom for differences of Christian opinion could be allowed, and a firm emphasis on predestination repudiated. In this way those who have been called the *Caroline Divines* are the forerunners not only of the Oxford Movement of the nineteenth century but also of the Deism of the eighteenth century.

(*a*) *Arminian Theology and High Church Principles in England.* One of the theologians whom James I had sent to the Synod of Dort was Dr. Davenant, then head of a Cambridge College, who later became Bishop of Salisbury. He may be taken as an example of the then dominant Calvinism. He wrote an answer to a treatise on God's love to mankind, in which he admitted that God has a general love to mankind, but insisted on the danger of magnifying this common love. It might obscure that special love which God had from all eternity for his chosen. He admitted that predestination, if it means anything, carries reprobation with it.

On the other side, Richard Montagu, afterwards Bishop of Chichester, wrote a defence of the Church of England in reply to a tract called *A Gagg for the new Gospel.* His defence was entitled *A Gagg for the New Gospel? No: A New Gagg for an Old Goose.* He repudiated the idea that the beliefs that by the fall of Adam man lost his free-will, and that faith once possessed can never be lost, were doctrines of the Church of England. He called the framers of the strongly Calvinistic Lambeth Articles of 1595 Puritans. As the committee which

framed them was presided over by Archbishop John Whitgift, Montagu's dissent is a sign of the change in attitude
which was coming over the Church of England.

The opposition is connected with the growth of the High
Church party which began with a sermon preached against
the Puritans by Richard Bancroft (1544–1610), then chap-
lain to Archbishop Whitgift, at St. Paul's Cross, in February
1588. Bancroft (who became Archbishop of Canterbury
(1604–10), but had effective power from 1597) proclaimed the
divine right of government by bishops.

William Laud (1573–1645; Archbishop of Canterbury
1633–45) developed Bancroft's theory of episcopacy, uniting
with it a stress on Patristic Christology and on the real
presence in the Eucharist, and an attitude which was in a
broad sense Arminian. He was a busy administrator rather
than a theologian; but we find in him an element that fore-
shadowed the seventeenth-century latitudinarian attitude,
which was to prove unstable in the eighteenth century. In this
reason is given a wide freedom, but the priority of Revelation
and the incapacity of reason to measure it are assumed. So
he writes: 'The Books called the Scriptures are commonly
and constantly reputed to be the Word of God, and so infallible verity to the least point of them. Doth any man
doubt this? The world cannot keep him from going to weigh
it at the balance of reason, whether it be the Word of God or
not. To the same weights he brings the Tradition of the
Church, the inward motives in Scripture itself, all testimonies
within which seem to bear witness to it; and in all this there
is no harm. The danger is when a man will use no other scale
but reason, or prefer reason before any other scale. For the
Word of God, and the Book containing it, refuse not to be
weighed by reason. But the scale is not large enough to
contain, nor the weights to measure out, the true virtue and
full force of either. Reason, then, can give no supernatural
ground into which a man may resolve his faith that Scripture
is the Word of God infallibly; yet reason can go so high, as it
can prove that Christian Religion, which rests upon the

authority of this Book, stands upon surer grounds of nature, reason, common equity, and justice, than anything in the world which any infidel or mere naturalist hath done, doth, or can adhere unto, against it, in that which he makes, accounts, or assumes as religion to himself.'[1]

Richard Baxter (1615–91), that most ecumenically minded of Christians, helped to undermine Calvinism by maintaining it in such a form that its rigours were softened. To Baxter, Christ died for all men, but not equally. He died for the good of all, and ordained the elect to faith, perseverance and glory. The glass in which we are to know God is our own soul, where we may see his image. Our conceptions of him may be inadequate, but they are true. Our knowledge of him is that which we have on the human side, and by this we must reason.

Baxter claims our attention for his discussion of the evidences of Christianity. In the second part of *The Saint's Everlasting Rest* (1650) he complained of a custom which had arisen among the Puritans of resolving all into the testimony of the Spirit. But the Spirit did not give men eyes. It only opened the eyes which men already possess. The reason has to be rectified, purified, illuminated, and then the evidence of the truth of Christianity is invincible. For the rectifying of reason there is need, not only of the Spirit's illumination but also of the Scriptures; for God reveals by His Spirit what is received in the Word, not independently of the Word but by giving his Spirit to illuminate our reason, to understand what is already revealed in the Scriptures. Baxter's conception of the 'rectification' of reason, in the very process of using it with full integrity, deserves consideration outside its seventeenth-century setting.

(*b*) *Rational Theology.* Characteristic of the seventeenth century is the appeal to reason without carrying out to the end the implications of that appeal. This can be seen first in *William Chillingworth* (1602–44), who became a Roman

[1] Text in *Anglicanism*, P. E. More and F. L. Cross (eds.), S.P.C.K., 1935, pp. 102–3.

Catholic, but afterwards returned to his first allegiance to the Church of England. His *Religion of Protestants a sure way of salvation* was an attempt to find a common ground for toleration. His saying, '*The Bible*, I say, *the Bible* only, is the Religion of Protestants', was meant as a formula of comprehensiveness. Protestants, he thought, will be made one, if they make no more demands upon one another than what they hold in common, that is, the Bible. But the basis on which he came to this conviction was a confidence in the duty of seeking truth and in the fact of finding it. 'This is the religion which I have chosen after a long deliberation,' he says, 'and I am very persuaded that I have chosen wisely, much more wisely than if I had guided myself according to your Church's authority' (R. of P. vi. 59).

He was in the long run widely influential and that in two ways. In the first place, he intended to submit exegetical questions to reasoned discussion. In the second place, he turned away from the conception of absolute truth to the conception of moral certainty.

Bishop *Jeremy Taylor* (1613–67) was another of those who, in appealing to Reason as the judge of divine things, started something that would lead farther than he would have liked. He is best known for his devotional works and would have preferred to be remembered for his casuistry; but he is important in the perspective of 1600–1965 for his *Discourse on the Liberty of Prophesying* (1647) in which he advocated religious toleration. Though he questioned the doctrine of Original Sin and incurred the suspicion of Pelagianism, and denied absolute Predestination and the damnation of unbaptized infants, he was substantially orthodox, and insisted on the Laudian doctrine of episcopacy.

But he called attention in his beautiful complex style to the uncertainty to be found in theological statements. 'The obscurity of some questions, the nicety of some articles, the intricacy of some revelations, the variety of humane understandings, the windings of logic . . . the several degrees of probability, the difficulties of Scripture, the invalidity of

probation of tradition, the opposition of all exterior arguments to each other, and their open contestation . . . have
made it impossible for any man in so great variety of matter
not to be deceived. No man pretends to it but the Pope, and
no man is more deceived than he is in that very particular.'[1]

Yet Jeremy Taylor is moderate in his claims for the reason
to which he appeals. 'Whatsoever is against right reason,' he
says, 'that no faith can oblige us to believe. For although
reason is not the positive and affirmative measure of our
faith, and God can do more than we can understand, and our
faith ought to be larger than our reason, and take something
into her heart that reason can never take into her eye; yet in
all our creed, there can be nothing against reason.'[2]

(c) *The Cambridge Platonists*. The Cambridge Platonists
are an interesting group of thinkers, who revolted against
contending dogmatisms and grasped at a premature synthesis
of Reason and Revelation. They were not widely influential
in their own time, but added something to the atmosphere
which the eighteenth century inherited.

Their favourite text was 'The spirit of man is the candle of
the Lord' (Prov. 20:27) and they saw the mind of man at its
best harmonizing the whole of human life in the service of
God. In this they emphasized morality and dedication of
spirit rather than theological dogma. So in their very appeal
to reason they turned away from intellectualism to stress
action and feeling rather than abstract reflection. Thus they
provide a vision of the unity of Reason, Revelation and
Christian living, without solving the problems involved.

Benjamin Whichcote (1609–83) was the teacher of the
group. He saw in Reason the test of Scripture, maintained
that some questions, on which good men disagreed, were
insoluble, and pleaded for freedom of thought. John Smith
(1616–52) insisted that our share in the divine light by which
alone we see divine things is conditioned by our advance in
the divine life. Ralph Cudworth (1617–88) was the most

---

[1] L. of P., 1647, p. 191.
[2] *The Worthy Communicant*, 1660, p. 244.

learned of the group. He taught that 'the Intelligible Ideas' are external and necessary modes of the divine mind, and that through them God enables us both to understand the universe and also to respond to God himself.

Nathaniel Culverwell (1618–51) is the only one of the group who showed an unresolved tension between testing everything by the light of reason and accepting Biblical statements when they are dark to reason. Henry More (1614–87) above all stressed the cleansing of the heart by the operation of the Holy Spirit so that with it, too, the reason is cleansed. Peter Sterry (d. 1672) was the mystic of the group. He saw the universe in the light of God in Christ as an emancipation proceeding by various stages of darkness and light from God to God.

(d) *Latitudinarianism in Preaching.* John Tillotson (1630–94) who at the end of his life (1691–4) became Archbishop of Canterbury, was a notable and widely influential preacher. He held to traditional doctrines, but did not make them the subject of his preaching.

Tillotson dwelt on the moral constitution of man. He stressed the necessity and blessedness of being righteous, and the worthlessness of all religious acts that were divorced from doing justly and loving mercy. He held to the Christian Revelation in the old sense as clear and undoubted. But this clearness and certainty have their foundation in Natural Religion, to which the Christian Revelation is an addition. Faith is simply a persuasion of the mind concerning anything. No Revealed Religion can overthrow the Natural, and natural precepts have a greater claim than those of any positive religion.

While Tillotson insists that the Old Testament prophecies are fulfilled in Christ, he stresses the miracles as the chief evidence for the authority of both Moses and Jesus. We have the credible report of eyewitnesses, which ought to be sufficient for our belief.

(e) *Isaac Newton* (1642–1727). The importance of Isaac Newton for the history of Christian theology is not his private religious convictions but the implications of his scientific achievement. In his *Philosophiae Naturalis Principia Mathematica* (1687) he showed by mathematical demonstration that the movements of the heavenly bodies are explicable by gravitation. This altered the whole climate of European reflection. The physical universe became for thinking minds a realm of law interpretable by mechanical cause and effect.

To Newton belief in God and his Providence depends chiefly on the wonderful order of the universe; but a later age may think either that God can have no activity within that wonderful order, or even that that order is self-explanatory. For all theologians, Newton's discoveries provided a new context in which Christian theology had now to be affirmed.

(*f*) *John Locke* (1603–1704). John Locke focuses the seventeenth century halfway position between a thorough appeal to reason, and an acceptance of Revelation as beyond the scrutiny of reason. Although he acknowledged that some truths are above reason, he insisted that reason must be our best judge and guide in all things, and he applied this to the understanding of Revelation.

In *The Reasonableness of Christianity as delivered in the Scriptures* (1695) he both drastically simplified Christian doctrine and acknowledged mysteries that were above reason. The essence of Christianity is, he thought, belief in Christ as the Messiah, one sent from God to reveal his true nature, and a life in accordance with Christian morality. God's mercy and grace are qualities which our reason would have revealed to us in time, and the morality of the New Testament is strictly in accordance with human reason.

In this simplification of Christian truth Locke omits the doctrine of the Trinity from the list of reasonable doctrines, and displaces the Cross from its central position. On the other hand, he still believes in the Virgin Birth and in the Resurrection. He also accepts the miracles. We believe the Christian faith on the credit of Jesus of Nazareth, and the outward signs which make such belief reasonable are his fulfilment of the prophecies about the Messiah and his performance of miracles.

Locke, in fact, was either too conservative or too radical, and he bequeathed this problem to the eighteenth century.

II.—THE EIGHTEENTH CENTURY

CHRISTIAN THEOLOGY IN A WORLD NEWLY FREE TO THINK
FOR ITSELF

General Characteristics

The eighteenth century was both the century of the
Enlightenment and the century of the discovery of the
importance of human feeling. It represents a watershed in
the history of mankind, and there can be no going back
behind it. Here man became of age, mature, able to think for
himself without ecclesiastical tutelage. Whatever difficulties
this causes for Christian faith and Christian theology, it
needs to be welcomed, because it has added to the dignity of
human life. The question of how to use this new-found
maturity is the continuing problem.

Immanuel Kant in his famous essay *What is Enlightenment?* (1784) said: 'Enlightenment is man's exodus from his
self-incurred immaturity. Immaturity is the inability to use
one's understanding without the guidance of another person.
This tutelage is self-incurred and its cause lies not in any
weakness of the understanding, but in indecision and lack of
courage to raise the mind without the guidance of someone
else. "Dare to know? Have the courage to use your own understanding; this is the mother of the Enlightenment." '[1] He
took only a modest view of how far his own age had shown the
freedom necessary to enter into its opportunities and said, 'If
the question is asked: Do we now live in an enlightened age?
the answer is: No, but certainly in an age of Enlightenment.'

In the eighteenth century there was an attempt to judge

[1] *Works*, H. Hartenstein (ed.), IV, pp. 159–68.

everything by the standard of human reason, and initially
to believe that the universal principles of human reason were
universally held. Revelation was not ruled out, but its
particularistic emphasis could only be a reinforcement of
what was known by reason. In any case right conduct was
far more important than right belief. It was an age characterized more by clarity than by profundity; its very moralism
prevented it probing the deeper mysteries. But its fundamental approach cannot be set aside.

In the course of the century the difficulties of this appeal to
reason became clear, as well as the difficulties of the evidence
for Revelation, and there was an inclination to find the nature
of man not in his reason but in his instincts and emotions.
The emphasis on feeling is equally with intellectualism a
characteristic of the eighteenth century. In both respects,
and in its probing in an abstract way the nature of historical
evidence, it paved the way for the nineteenth century.

1. *Orthodoxy*

Orthodoxy in the eighteenth century continued to be
under the Islamic domination of the Turks. In this situation
it maintained a thoroughly conservative attitude in order to
preserve its heritage intact. It also suffered from the fact
that the theological students of ability could only find
adequate training in Western Schools and inevitably used
Roman Catholic or Protestant methods and approach which
made them out of touch with the life of Orthodoxy.

The most interesting episode was the attempt by the Non-
Jurors, that group of Anglican divines who felt themselves
so bound by their oath of allegiance to James II that they
could not accept William and Mary and so went out of the
Church of England, to establish relations with both Greek
and Russian Orthodox Churches. The correspondence lasted
from 1716 to 1725. It reveals the complete incomprehension
by each side of the position of the other. The Anglicans on
their part wanted the Orthodox to give up the direct invoca-
tion of the saints, the veneration of ikons, the adoration of

the eucharistic elements and the special devotion to the Mother of God. The Orthodox were prepared to explain their position, but were firm. They hardly understood the position of their correspondents, and found them steeped, as they thought, in Luthero-Calvinist principles and prejudices. But the contact may have been fruitful for future approaches.

2. *Catholicism*

In the eighteenth century Catholic theology may be said to have reached the nadir of its whole history. A sign of this is to be found in the fact that on the 8th June 1773 Pope Clement XIV yielded to political pressure, and signed the Brief *Dominus Ac Redemptor* which suppressed the Society of Jesus. Catholic apologists tended to undermine their own position by accepting many of the rationalist presuppositions of the time. Voltaire, that redoubtable product and enemy of Catholicism, said when he heard of the suppression: 'In twenty years there will be nothing left of the Church.' He was wrong, but his instinct was right in seeing in it a weakening of the Catholic will to survive.

In Catholic theology of the period there was a purely defensive attitude. The atmosphere is the general debate of the time. The French Enlightenment in particular declared open war on religious claim to validity and truth. Voltaire (François-Marie Arouet (1694–1778)), with his courage, vague theism and deep pessimism, and his violent opposition to the Catholic Church represents one reaction to Catholicism; Jean-Jacques Rousseau (1712–78), who swivelled between Calvinism and Catholicism, and preached a sentimental Deism, but generally refrained from attacking the Catholic Church, represents another. It was not till the nineteenth century that Catholic theology began to recover life and power.

3. *The Main Debate*

(a) *The Heritage of Locke.* The eighteenth century started where Locke left off. He had developed his empirical philosophy and propounded a simplified dogmatic. For the authority of tradition, he had substituted experience and freedom of enquiry. 'Reason,' he said, 'must be our last judge and guide in all things,' (*Essay*, IV, 19, 14). In so saying he had given an overwhelming prestige to Natural Religion which the eighteenth century proceeded to develop. Locke's simplified statement of Revelation was the conclusion he arrived at. This was where the eighteenth century started. It proceeded to ask whether there was any need for Revelation and if so what were its credentials.

Locke also bequeathed to the eighteenth century a hostility to *enthusiasm*. 'Enthusiasm,' Locke said, 'takes away both reason and revelation, and substitutes in the room of it the ungrounded fancies of a man's own brain, and assumes them for a foundation both of opinion and conduct' (*Essay*, IV, 19, 3).

(*b*) *Natural Religion Alone*. The heritage of Locke led to the argument that the universal God must lay his universal demands upon man through reason alone and not through the positive tenets of a specific revelation. This argument had really been started by Lord Herbert of Cherbury (1543–1648) particularly in his *De Religione Gentilium* (1663). He held that common to all religions were five innate ideas: (i) that there is a God; (ii) that he ought to be worshipped; (iii) that virtue is the chief element in this worship; (iv) that repentance for sin is a duty; (v) that there is another life of rewards and punishments. But his views were taken up in a volume called *The Oracles of Reason* by Charles Blount (1654–93) published posthumously in 1693.

The argument is summed up in *Christianity as old as the Creation* by Matthew Tindal (1657–1733), published in 1730. This is a sustained affirmation that the law of reason given in the nature of things is absolutely perfect; anything additional to it is arbitrary; anything contrary to it is false; the Bible is only authoritative in so far as its contents are approved by reason.

By Natural Religion he understood the belief in the existence of a God, and the awareness and performance of

the duties which we know through our knowledge by reason
of the perfections of God, our own imperfections, and our
relation to God and our fellow-creatures. It is founded on the
reason and nature of things (p. 11). This involves obedience
to the *Law of Nature or Reason*, which is common or natural
to all rational creatures. This, like God, is absolutely perfect
and unchangeable. True Christianity is not something
recent, but what God at the beginning dictated, and still
continues to dictate, to Christians, as well as to others
(pp. 7–8). It is, he thought, evident by the light of Nature
that there is a God, that is, a Being absolutely perfect
and infinitely happy in himself, who is the source of all
other beings (p. 11). True religion is a constant disposition
of mind to do all the good we can, and so make ourselves
acceptable to God by fulfilling the purpose of his creation
(p. 18).

Natural Religion differs from *Revealed* only in the way it is
communicated. The one is the internal, the other is the
external revelation of the unchangeable will of a being who is
always infinitely wise and good (p. 2).

In the course of his sustained affirmation of the perfection
of Natural Religion, and of its corollary that Christianity
is only a republication of that perfection, Tindal gave a
running criticism of any understanding of Revelation that
made it not identical with Natural Religion. On this basis
God would be an arbitrary being (p. 26 and elsewhere), and
not the perfect unchangeable Being we worship. Also God
would be promulgating two different laws having authority
at the same time (p. 117). To suppose that anything can be
true by Revelation which is false by reason is to undermine
Revelation, because nothing unreasonable can come from the
God of universal reason (p. 158). What it concerns men to
know above all else, must certainly be knowable by every
man (p. 267). If mankind could not know God and their duty
to him apart from *additional* light from the Christian Revelation, God would have left the whole of mankind for four
thousand years, and the greater part of it still at the present

time without sufficient means to know or do their duty (p. 339). But all this is quite impossible.

In Tindal's longest chapter (the thirteenth) he discusses the difficulties of understanding what the Bible means (including problems of text and translation and of the kind of language used in the Bible). He also considers the difficulties of deciding what commands are binding on us when we have found out the meaning. The only way to solve all these difficulties is to appeal to universal reason.

The Christian Gospel is the republication of that religion which is founded on the eternal reason of things. That Natural Religion still governs us—'since we are obliged to recede from *the letter*, though the words are ever so plain, if that recedes from the Reason of things; as all own *the letter* does, in innumerable places relating to God himself; by imputing human parts, human infirmities and human passions, even of the worst kind, to him, and making those the cause of many of his actions. And that as in the *Old Testament* there are several things, either commanded, or approved, which would be criminal in us to observe, because we can't reconcile our doing them with the Reason of things; so in the *New Testament*, its precepts are for the most part delivered either so hyperbolically, that they would lead men astray, were they governed by the usual meaning of words, or else expressed in so loose, general and undetermined a manner that men are as much left to be governed by the Reason of things as if there were no such precepts: and the Scripture not distinguishing between those precepts which are occasional, and which are not, we have no ways to distinguish them, but from the Nature of things, which will point out to us those rules which eternally oblige, whether delivered in Scripture or not' (pp. 318–19).

Tindal expresses succinctly the difference between his own position and that of those such as Dr. Samuel Clarke who oppose it: 'The difference between those who would engross the name of Christians to themselves, and these *Christian Deists*, as I may justly call them: is, that the former dare not

D

examine into the truth of Scripture-Doctrines lest they seem
to question the veracity of the Scriptures: whereas the latter
who believe not the Doctrines because contained in Scripture,
but the Scriptures on account of the Doctrines, are under no
such apprehension. For having critically examined those
Doctrines by that reason, which God has given them to
distinguish religion from superstition, they are sure not to
run into errors of moment; notwithstanding the confessed
obscurity of the Scriptures, and those many mistakes that
have crept into the text, whether by accident or design'
(p. 336).

(c) *What Historical Evidence is there for Christianity?* The
Deists argued against the need for a specific Revelation. But
granted there was a function for a specific Revelation to
fulfil, did the evidence for Christianity show it to be the
Revelation that was needed?

The eighteenth century prepared the ground for the great
development of historical enquiry in the nineteenth, by its
probing in an abstract way, the nature of historical evidence.
In 1722 William Whiston's book: *An Essay towards restoring
the true text of the Old Testament, and for indicating the
citations made thence in the New Testament* stressed the convincing nature and general satisfactoriness of the proof from
prophecy. But in 1724 Anthony Collins retorted with *A
Discourse on the Grounds and Reasons of the Christian Religion.*
In this he agreed with Whiston that prophecy is the only
proof of the divine origin of Christianity, but denied that
prophecy and fulfilment ever correspond.

In 1727–9 Thomas Woolston developed the other side of
the controversy by writing a series of tracts in which he
applied an allegorical interpretation to the miracles and
denied that they had any value as testimonies to the divine
mission of Christ. The most important of the replies to
Woolston was Bishop Sherlock's *Trial of the Witnesses* (1729).
He certainly demolished Woolston's contention that Jesus
and his disciples conspired to deceive.

The attack on the miracles was taken further by David

Hume in his *Essay on Miracles* published in 1748. In this he argued against finding miracles independent evidence for divine revelation. 'It is experience only', he said, 'which gives authority to human testimony, and it is the same experience which assures us of the laws of nature. . . . No human testimony can have such a force as to prove a miracle, and make it a just foundation for a system of religion.' Hume had argued that reason was unable to find any intellectual grounds for our belief in causes and laws, but he is not concerned with consistency but with demolition of a position. He ends his essay with an insistence that reason can have nothing to do with miracles. 'Upon the whole,' he said acidly, 'we may conclude that the Christian religion not only was at first attended with miracles, but even at this day cannot be believed without one. Mere reason is sufficient to convince us of its veracity. And whoever is moved *by faith* to assent to it is conscious of a continued miracle in his own person which subverts all the principles of his understanding and gives him a determination to believe what is most contrary to custom and experience.' This is in fact a denial that miracles are a living intellectual possibility. Certainly after this it is no use appealing to miracles as a *demonstration* to the unbeliever that the Christian Revelation is true.

In 1794 William Paley published the first edition of his *View of the Evidence of Christianity*. Paley was no original thinker, but he was a splendid expositor. The book is the summing up of the discussion in a positive direction. Paley concentrated on the miracles and relegated prophecy to one of the auxiliary evidences. But before he developed his argument he had a preliminary chapter on the antecedent credibility of miracles. In this he said (p. 3): 'This is the prejudication we would resist. For this length does a modern objection to miracles go, *viz.* that no human testimony can in any case render them credible. I think the reflection above stated that, if there be a revelation, there must be miracles, and that, under the circumstances in which the human species are placed, a revelation is not improbable, or not improbable

in any great degree, to be a fair answer to the whole objection.'
Paley has gone to the root of the matter here, though he did
not himself establish a sound position. Since the Enlightenment, the Christian theologian must establish if not to the
satisfaction of all, at least to the satisfaction of some, honestly
grappling with the questions, that there is some antecedent
probability of what he affirms.

Paley's main argument was that there is reliable evidence
in Christianity as not in other religions that the original
witnesses of miracles suffered greatly in order to be faithful
to their account, and submitted to new rules of conduct. He
declared that Christianity was from the beginning a miraculous story, which depends on the authority of Scripture. He
then argued in a long chapter with eleven sections that the
New Testament consists of accredited historical documents.
This was a careful piece of work and paved the way towards
a consideration of what the documents say and how their
content can be used in historical reconstruction.

In Part II, *The Auxiliary evidences of Christianity*, Paley's
main points concern prophecy (stressing Isaiah 53 and
Christ's prediction of the fall of Jerusalem); the History of the
Resurrection (which he says was obviously not a product of
mere enthusiasm), and the evidence to be seen in the propa-
gation of Christianity which shows that 'a Jewish peasant
overthrew the religion of the world' (p. 345).

In addition he tried to meet some popular objections. He
was not prepared for Christianity to take any more responsibility for the Old Testament than to follow Christ in assuming
the divine origin of the Mosaic institution, and in recognizing
the prophetic character of many of the ancient Jewish
writers (pp. 354, 355). Against the characteristically
eighteenth-century criticism of the lack of necessary truth in
the Christian revelation, Paley argued that 'irresistible proof
would restrain the voluntary powers too much; would not
answer the purpose of trial and probation, would call from us
no exercise of candour, seriousness, humility, inquiry; no submission of passion, interests and prejudices, to moral evidence

and to probable truth; no habits of reflection; none of that previous desire to learn and to obey the will of God, which forms perhaps the test of the virtuous principle' (pp. 386, 387).

Further in criticism of the pressure for overpowering evidence in a revelation, Paley turned at length to *internal evidence:* 'which ought, perhaps, to bear a considerable part in the proof of every revelation, because it is a species of evidence which applies itself to the knowledge, love, and practice, of virtue, and which operates in proportion to the degree of those qualities which it finds in the person whom it addresses. Men of good dispositions, amongst Christians, are greatly affected by the impression which the Scriptures themselves make upon their minds' (p. 387).

Finally, he insisted that critics often look for the influence of religion in the wrong place, and charge Christianity with many consequences for which it is not responsible (p. 390). He also said: 'differences of opinion, when accompanied with mutual charity, which Christianity forbids them to violate, are for the most part innocent, and for some purposes useful. They promote inquiry, discussion, and knowledge. They help to keep up an attention to religious subjects, and a concern about them, which might be apt to die away in the calm and silence of universal agreement' (p. 397).

The nineteenth century was to probe much more searchingly into the question of the historical evidence of Christianity, but this probing starts from the position reached in the eighteenth century.

(*d*) *No historical evidence can prove the truth of Christianity.* Gotthold Ephraim Lessing (1729–81) was one of those figures who, though rooted in their own environment, obscurely sense changes that are likely to take place, and, by the striking character of the way they write, call attention to the underlying problems. He is important primarily for two things. On the one hand, he focused an uncertainty about the relation of historical facts to the eternal truth of God. On the other hand, he asserted that there is a progressive educative process in the history of mankind. The change from thinking of the Christian Gospel as Revelation to thinking of it as the Historic Faith has its root in Lessing.

The first theme is strikingly asserted in Lessing's famous Tract *On the proof of the Spirit and Power*.[1] Lessing argued that reports of historical truths are only as reliable as historical truths ever can be. 'If no historical truth can be demonstrated then nothing can be demonstrated by means of historical truths. That is: *accidental truths of history can never become the proof of necessary truths of reason.*'

In Lessing's argument the main questions which are intertwined are these: 1—What kind of trustworthiness can be given to historical truth? Is it less trustworthy because it is not demonstrative as mathematics is? 2—How can historical truth be linked with present conviction of the eternal truth of God? 3—Is theological truth intrinsically unreasonable? Whatever the right answer may be to these questions, Lessing certainly bequeathed to a large section of German Protestant theology in particular a lack of confidence in historical fact.

Lessing's second theme was developed in his last published work, *The Education of the Human Race* (1780). He asserted that 'what education is to the individual man, revelation is to the whole human race' (§ 1). 'Education gives man nothing which he could not also get from within himself. It gives him that which he could get from within himself, only more quickly and more easily. In the same way too, revelation gives nothing to the human race which human reason could not arrive at on its own; only it has given and still gives to it the most important of these things sooner.' But towards the end of the book (§ 77), he thought that even by means of a religion of whose historical truth we may be dubious, we may be led to 'closer and better conceptions of the divine Being, of our own nature, of our own relation to God, which human reason would never have reached on its own'.

He saw the human race being led from polytheism and

[1] *Lessing's Theological Writings*, Henry Chadwick (ed.), A. and C. Black, 1956, pp. 51-6.

idolatry (which came about because human reason broke up
the one immeasurable into many measurables) to the
Revelation to the Jewish people, and from there to Christ,
the 'first *reliable, practical* teacher of the immortality of the
soul'. There remains still to come, and Lessing is certain that
it will come, the time of the perfecting when man will do
right because it is right, and not because arbitrary rewards
are set upon it. Nature must succeed with the whole, even
if it means that every individual man will have been present
more than once in the world. In this work there are the roots
both of the theory of progressive revelation, and of the science
of comparative religion.

(e) *Natural Religion is Not More Convincing than Revealed
Religion. Both are trustworthy in spite of the difficulties.* What
influence the *Analogy of Religion Natural and Revealed to the
Constitution and Cause of Nature* (1736) by Joseph Butler
(1692–1752) may have had on the eighteenth century we do
not really know—though it represents a logical negative
answer to Matthew Tindal's trust in a natural religion
which is perfect. The nineteenth century treated the *Analogy*
as a wonderful apologetic for Christianity: the twentieth
century wonders whether to take notice of it at all because it
is not convinced of Butler's assumptions. It is, however,
worth while to read it not only for its place in the eighteenth
century, but also as a hint, if no more than that, of how we
may trust the revelation of God which comes to us through
the general experience of life (in spite of its imperfections)
and also the revelation of God which comes to us specifically
through the Christian testimony (in spite of its imperfections).

Butler, himself, was quite specific about the limitations of
what he is attempting to do. He said: 'It is not the purpose
of this chapter, nor of this Treatise, properly to prove God's
perfect moral government over the world, or the truth of
Religion; but to observe what there is in the constitution and
cause of nature, to confirm the proper proof of it, supposed
to be known.'[1] At the end he thought that 'it has been shown

---

[1] *Works*, W. E. Gladstone (ed.), *The Analogy* I. iii (§ 32, p. 75).

that a serious apprehension that Christianity may be true, lays persons under the strictest obligations of a serious regard to it, throughout the whole of their life: a regard not the same exactly, but in many respects nearly the same, with what a full conviction of its truth would lay them under'.

His conclusion depends on the distinction he made between divine and human intelligence: 'For nothing which is the possible object of knowledge, whether past, present, or future can be probable to an infinite intelligence; since it cannot but be discerned absolutely as itself in itself, certainly true or certainly false. But to us probability is the very guide of life' (Introduction, § 4, p. 5). We must even act on a low probability, if that is the best judgment we can make. 'For surely a man is as really bound in prudence to do what upon the whole appears, according to the best of his judgment, to be for his happiness, as what he certainly knows to be so' (*ibid.*, p. 6). What Butler did not consider in his eighteenth-century setting is that different things may seem probable at different epochs.

In Part I *Of Natural Religion* Butler had three main concerns: a future life, the moral government of God, and the ignorance of man in relation to the immensity of God.

He did not think that a demonstrative proof of a future life would be a proof of religion. Atheism might still be true. He only thought that 'as religion implies a future state, any presumption against such a state, is a presumption against religion. But if a future life is taken as established to a very considerable degree of probability', belief in it 'would greatly open and dispose the mind seriously to attend to the general evidence of the whole' (I. i. § 32, p. 47). His principal arguments for a future life were that death may involve no greater change than the change from the womb to life, that observation proves that our body is no part of ourselves (the crucial point) and that mere apprehension to the contrary is of no weight.

The moral government of God Butler founded on his understanding of the moral nature which God has given us.

'For *first*, it is certain, that peace and delight, in some degree and upon some occasions, is the necessary and present effect of virtuous practice; and effect arising immediately from that constitution of our nature. We are so made, that well being as such gives us satisfaction, at least in some instances; ill-doing as such, in none. And *secondly*, from our moral nature, joined with God's having put our happiness and misery in many respects in each other's power, it cannot but be that vice as such, some kinds and instances of it at least, will be infamous, and men will be disposed to punish it as in itself detestable: and the villain will by no means be able always to avoid feeling that infamy, any more than he will be able to escape this further punishment, which mankind will be disposed to inflict upon him, under the notion of his deserving it' (I. iii, § 18, pp. 64–5).

Butler had a profound sense of the vast ignorance of man compared with the immensity of God. Assuming that God exercises a moral government over the world, it is natural to assume that the whole pattern of it must be beyond our comprehension. A full knowledge of that pattern would show reasons, interconnections and excellences that we cannot now see. We should find that the permission of disorders was perfectly compatible with justice and goodness (I, vii, § 22, pp. 143–4).

In Part II, 'Of Revealed Religion', Butler insisted that Christianity is not only an authoritative promulgation of the Law of Nature, it is also a revelation of a particular dispensation of Providence, for the recovery and salvation of mankind from a state of ruin. In fact we accept God as the Governor of the world, upon the evidence of reason; and that Christ is the Mediator between God and man, and the Holy Spirit our Guide and Sanctifier, upon the evidence of revelation (II. i, §§ 15–18, pp. 162–3).

The crucial question about the Revelation was whether it is historically true. The question as Butler saw it is whether the history is the product of honest minds or whether it is fictitious, and in these terms he rightly asserts historical genuineness. It had to be left to a later generation to probe more deeply the complex question, what constitutes historical truth.

The question that Butler raised about miracles in the historical evidence is whether there is any special presumption against miracles. Butler insisted that there is a presumption of millions to one against the most ordinary facts before they are established. And he asks: 'What can a small presumption, additional to this, amount to, though it be peculiar?' (II. ii, § 12, p. 180). Butler here is open to the later criticism of J. S. Mill that he has confused improbability before the fact (which is almost unlimited) and improbability after the fact (in which there is vast difference in probability between miracles and ordinary facts).

Of special interest is Butler's upholding of the appeal to reason. He thought, it is true, that we are likely to be incompetent judges of Revelation to a great degree, but he is very anxious not to belittle the function of reason itself, within its own proper sphere.

'I express myself with caution,' he said, 'lest I should be mistaken to vilify reason; which is indeed the only faculty we have wherewith to judge anything, even revelation itself; or be misunderstood to assert, that a supposed revelation cannot be proved false, from internal characters. For it may contain clear immoralities or contradictions; and either of these would prove it false. Nor will I take upon me to affirm that nothing else can possibly render any supposed revelation incredible.' Yet still it is true 'that objections against Christianity, as distinguished from objections against its evidence are frivolous' (II. iii, §§ 2, 3, p. 183) (cp. II. ix, § 7, p. 307, where he again spoke about not vilifying reason 'which is *the candle of the Lord* within us' (Prov. 20:27): though he went on to say that 'it can afford no light, where it does not shine; nor judge where it has no principles to judge upon').

Butler quite specifically upheld the right of reason to judge the meaning, the morality and the evidence of scripture.

'And now,' he asked, 'what is the just consequence from all these things?' Not that reason is no judge of what is offered to us as being of divine revelation. For this would be to infer that we are unable to judge of anything, because we are unable to judge of all things. Reason can, and ought to, judge not only of the meaning but also of the morality and the evidence of revelation. But his conclusion was: 'I know nothing of this sort objected against scripture, excepting such objections as are formed upon suppositions, which would equally conclude, that the constitution of nature is contradictory to wisdom, justice or goodness; which most certainly it is not' (II. iii, § 26, p. 196).

Here there are two points of importance. First Butler was assuming with his readers that Nature testifies clearly to the wisdom, justice and goodness of God. He has nothing specific to say to a later generation that wants to know how, starting without assumptions, you arrive at the conviction of the goodness and Lordship of God. Secondly, in Butler's caveat that reason can afford no light, where it does not shine, is a pointer to the fact that reason, without losing its critical character, needs to be transformed by Christian understanding before it can do justice to Christian truth.

(*f*) *But Why Should We Believe in Either Natural Religion or Revealed Religion?* A more radical answer to the confidence in Natural Religion alone came from David Hume (1663–1727) whose incisive argument showed the limits of what can be affirmed on the basis of reasoning alone, and who, out of a hostility to Christianity showed himself very dubious about any miraculous evidence. His main services to Christian theology come from the fact that he raised the question 'What can the mind know?' in a form which allows for no retreat, that he showed conclusively the limitations of the argument from design, and that he pioneered the study of the history of religion.

Hume wrote on religion from the standpoint of the detached observer. His own position was that of the urbane uncommitted man, who can afford to be tolerant, trusts in custom, sees in morals what is to the advantage of society, and believes that feelings rather than reason move men. In this stance there is expressed his deep revulsion from the Calvinism in which he was brought up. As a result he thinks that most Christians are hypocrites, and prefers a traditional mythological religion to a systematic scholastic one, because it makes no deep impression on the affections and the understanding (*The Natural History of Religion*, XII).

The argument for design in Hume's hands resolves itself into 'one simple though somewhat ambiguous, at least undefined proposition, that *the cause or causes of order in the universe probably bear some remote analogy to human intelligence*'; coupled with the reflection that 'as the works of nature have a much greater analogy to the effects of *our* art and contrivance, than to those of *our* benevolence and justice; we have reason to infer that the natural attributes of the Deity have a greater resemblance to those of man, than his morals have to human virtues'.[1]

Hume's *Essay on Miracles* is important not because it is a convincing argument against miracles (for it is not), but because it is a convincing argument against expecting what are claimed to be miracles to be convincing proof to the unbeliever of the revelation of God. It is also a warning to be cautious in accepting what are claimed to be miracles since miracles abound among ignorant nations, the passions of surprise and wonder joined with religion lead to excesses, and miracles are claimed for many religions.

But it is his teaching on the nature of human thinking that is specially important, and in this particularly his discussion of cause and of personal identity. Knowledge, Hume held, is based upon impressions (i.e. perceptions) and ideas which are the images of impressions given in memory and imagination. On this basis, we never perceive a cause, and all that a cause can mean is that it is 'an object precedent and contiguous to another, and so united with it that the idea of the

---

[1] *Dialogues concerning Natural Religion*, Norman Kemp Smith (ed.), O.U.P., 1935, pp. 281, 270.

one determines the mind to form the idea of the other, and
the impression of the one to form "a more lively idea of the
other".[1] Hume asked himself 'how it is that even after all, we
retain a degree of belief, which is sufficient for our purposes,
either in philosophy or common life?'; and answers that
'nature breaks the face of all sceptical arguments in time, and
keeps them from having any considerable influence on the
understanding'.[2]

So too in relation to the self Hume insisted that when we
enter most intimately into what we call 'ourselves' we also
find a particular perception and are not aware of a principle
other than particular perceptions.[3]

Hume's attitude (bearing in mind that for prudential
reasons his attitude to theology is hinted at rather than fully
expressed) came out in the famous ending to his *Inquiry concerning Human Understanding* (published in 1748 as *Philosophical Essays*): 'Divinity or theology, as it proves the
existence of a deity and the immortality of souls, is composed
partly of reasoning concerning particular, partly concerning
general facts. It has a foundation in *reason* so far as it is
supported by experience. But its best and most solid
foundation is faith and divine revelation. Morals and
criticism are not so properly objects of the understanding as
of taste and sentiment. Beauty, whether moral or natural, is
felt more properly than perceived.

'When we run over libraries, persuaded of these principles,
what havoc must we make? If we take in our hand any
volume—of divinity or school encyclopaedia, for instance—
let us ask, *Does it contain any abstract reasoning concerning
quantity or number?* No. *Does it contain any experimental
reasoning concerning matter of fact and existence?* No. Commit
it then to the flames, for it can contain nothing but sophistry
and illusion.'

This is a searching statement of the limitations of the
human mind in so far as it bases itself purely on argument.

[1] *A Treatise of Human Nature*, 1739–40, Book I, Part III, Section xiv.
[2] *Ibid.*, Part IV, Section i.   [3] *Ibid.*, Part IV, Section vi.

Unless there is a conception of human thinking which is open to aesthetic, moral and religious insight, then Christian theology is at an end, except on such terms as outrage human reason.

(g) *What Grasp Can We Have of Transcendent Reality?* Immanuel Kant (1724–1804) found himself woken out of his 'dogmatic slumber' by Hume, and accepted the fact that we must have a critical attitude to our powers of knowing. To understand the importance of Kant for Christian theology we must look at his work as a whole. It is his total perspective that matters.

In his *Critique of Pure Reason* (1781, 2nd edn. 1787) he set himself to work out a theory of knowledge which would provide a justification for Newtonian Science. He accepted Hume's judgment about the limitations on what we actually perceive, but he insisted that the mind supplies the categories by which we rationally order the material of our perception. The very constitution of the mind is such that its only source of genuine knowledge lies in this ordering of the data of perception by the categories of the understanding.

There are ideas which continually arise in the mind—the soul as a permanent substantial subject, the world as the totality of causally related phenomena, and God as absolute perfection—as the unity of the conditions of thought in general; but, according to Kant, we have no intellectual intuition of these ideas because they cannot be found as objective within perceptive experience. By so limiting knowledge Kant hoped to establish it on an unshakeable basis.

On the basis, then, of his theory Kant criticized the proofs by speculative reason for the existence of God. The *ontological* argument he set aside because it is absurd to introduce into the conception of a thing, the concept of its existence. The *cosmological* argument is unconvincing because the concept of *cause* only applies to the empirical world. All that the physico-theological argument can show is that we can infer from the order and design *visible* in the universe, the existence of a proportionate cause but not a creator of the world.

But besides the relation in which the understanding stands to objects in theoretical knowledge, Kant thought it also had a relation to the will. And in *The Critique of Practical Reason* (1788) he insisted on the absolute claim of the moral law which completely justifies its objective reality without any empirical intuition. Here is the heart of Kant's thinking. To him the claim of the 'ought' was ultimate and self-explanatory, and distinguished from every other experience. It had to do with the whole life of man. And this sense of duty implies freedom, God and immortality. For the sense of duty needs God to vindicate it, by effecting in a future life, as he clearly does not in this, a coincidence of justice and happiness.

In the *Critique of Judgment* (1790) Kant explored aspects of existence that seem to fall in an intermediate position between theoretical and moral knowledge. He endeavours to understand the element of purposiveness, which always impressed him, first in the sphere of fine art and then in the sphere of animal life.

Finally, in his *Religion within the Limits of Reason Alone* (1793) Kant expressed his profound sense of a radical evil in human life and of the need to combat it by a steadfast moral will, which alone can overcome it. If a man keeps his moral will free from impure elements and allows it to govern his life he will become convinced that the forces of evil are powerless to destroy it. Kant upholds Christianity in so far, but only in so far, as it is a symbolic representation of the religion of morality. To him the history of religion was a record of the conflict of the religion of outward worship with the religion of our duty to our neighbour. The only true means of grace is a morally good life. The performance of acts of prayer is to be deprecated.

What shall we say, then? Has Kant given a satisfactory answer to the problem posed by Hume; can the human mind grasp transcendent reality? The answer has two sides. On the one hand, Christian theology is immensely grateful to Kant for moving the discussion to a plane where Christian contentions begin to make sense. On the other hand, apart from his recessive individualism, his unhistorical approach, two aspects of his thinking have exercised a baleful influence. One is his negative approach to the task of metaphysics taken not merely as the end of a phase of the discussion but as the end of the discussion itself; and the other is his excessive moralism in the sphere of religion.

The nearness of Kant's approach to the Christian sphere of discussion may be illustrated by a passage towards the end of the *Critique of Judgment*.[1]

'Suppose the case of a man at the moment when his mind is disposed to a moral sensation. If surrounded by the beauties of nature, he is in a state of restful, serene enjoyment of his being, he feels a want, viz. to be grateful for this to some being or other. Or if another time he finds himself in the same state of mind when pressed by duties that he can and will only discharge by a voluntary sacrifice, he again feels in himself a want, viz. to have thus executed a command and obeyed a Supreme Lord. Or again: if he has in some heedless way transgressed his duty, but without becoming answerable to men, his severe self-reproach will speak to him with the voice of a judge to whom he has to give account. In a word, he needs a moral Intelligence, in order to have a Being for the purpose of his existence, which may be, conformably to this purpose, the cause of himself and of the world. It is vain to assign motives behind these feelings, for they are immediately connected with the purest moral sentiment, because *gratitude*, *obedience* and *humiliation* (submission to deserved chastisement) are mental dispositions that make for duty; and the mind which is inclined towards a widening of its moral sentiment here only voluntarily conceives an object which is not in the world where possible to render its duty before such an one.'

But the hurtful influence of Kant can be seen in two ways. The first concerns the task of the metaphysical theologian to grapple with the metaphysical ultimate. Kant himself said

[1] Appendix, § 86, J. H. Bernard (ed.), Macmillan, 1935, pp. 374–5.

that he had to remove knowledge to make room for faith; and up to a point the second *Critique* makes up for the negations of the first. But only up to a point. For one thing Kant's theory of knowledge does not explain the mind's grasp of the transcendent, and in doing justice to the formative character of the mind in knowledge, he minimized the way in which assertions of the mind are claims to be affirming what is in fact true. And the mysterious fact that we do grasp the transcendent in the form of truth has to be given due weight.

For another thing, Kant kept rigidly within the scheme of the first *Critique* and did not reconstruct his attitude to metaphysics in the light of the *Critique of Practical Reason*. Granted that metaphysics based purely on argument alone must be very limited in its scope, what if it is based on the awareness of the transcendent in morals and (though Kant would not allow it) in aesthetics and in religion? Kant is right in thinking that our awareness of the transcendent does not come from abstract thinking but from thinking in the context of the practical demands made upon it. But we need a fuller admission that the mind can really grasp the transcendent, even if we must admit that the articulation of what it does grasp will be, to use a thought of St. Thomas, only by a few, after a long time, and with many errors.

But Kant's moralism, for all its greatness, has been a stumbling block when Christian theologians have too slavishly followed it. Christian theology owes a deep debt to Kant for this vindication of the characteristic depth and claim of the moral experience, and for maintaining its essential independence against pressure from the state and from ecclesiastical institutions. But in so doing he was insensitive and up to a point hostile to the characteristic Christian experience of humbling but delivering grace. Such an experience needs to be held in tension with the absolute claim of obedience to duty. It cannot supersede it, but it can enrich it. But the grace of God is the main fact in Christian theology, from which moral transformation is only

E

a by-product of the rule of God in the hearts of men. Here
Kant's influence must be resisted. His insensitiveness to the
historic revelation and the importance of corporate institutions for both morality and religion also make him a bad
guide. The ambivalence of Kant needs full recognition.

(*h*) *The Reaffirmation of the Old Dogmatism in a New Form.*
Jonathan Edwards (1703–58) is a fascinating figure of the
eighteenth-century scene. He used his immense gifts of
philosophical analysis and beautiful prose in the science of a
Mystic Puritanism. He combined in himself a metaphysical
absolutism and an experimental temper that shows his eager
response to the scientific discoveries of Newton and to the
empirical philosophy of Locke. He attempted to do justice
both to the majesty of God and to the immediacy of his
presence.

His contribution to the movement of Christian Theology
consists primarily in his rearguard action in favour of the
absolute sovereignty of God—which serves as a warning of
the difficulty of finding an intellectually satisfying alternative
affirmation—and in the contribution he made to the appeal
to experience in his notable study of *Religious Affections*
(1746).

Edwards made clear his dominant concern for the absolute
sovereignty of God in his first published utterance 'God
Glorified in the Work of Redemption'. He expounded the
reality of God not only in terms of an absolute power but also
in terms of his absolute beauty by the Greatness of Men's
Dependence upon Him in the whole of it.[1]

What God aims at in the work of redemption is that man
should not glory in himself but only in God, and in it men are
absolutely and immediately dependent on him. All the good
that men have is in and through Christ who '*is made unto us
wisdom, righteousness, sanctification and redemption*'. God
has given us Christ, and it is of him that we are in Christ
Jesus by faith.

[1] Text in *Puritan Sage*, Nergilius Ferm (ed.), Library Publishers, New
York, 1953, pp. 144–56.

Though God is pleased to lift man out of the abyss again to a high pitch of glory and blessedness, yet he has nothing in any respect to glory in: all the glory plainly belongs to God. All schemes of divinity that oppose such an absolute and universal dependence on God derogate from his glory and thwart the design of our redemption.

Edwards finishes his sermon in this way: 'Hath any man hope that he is converted, and sanctified, and that his mind is converted and sanctified, and that his mind is endowed with true excellency and spiritual beauty? that his sins are forgiven, and he is received unto God's favour, and exalted to the honour and blessedness of being his child, and an heir of eternal life? let him give God all the glory; who alone makes him to differ from the worst of men in this world, or the most miserable of the damned in hell. Hath any man much comfort and strong hope of eternal life? let not his hope lift him up, but dispose him the more to abase himself, to reflect on his own exceeding unworthiness of such a favour, and to exalt God alone. Is any man eminent in holiness, and abundant in good works? let him take nothing of the glory of it to himself, but ascribe it to him whose "workmanship we are, created in Christ Jesus unto good works"' (p. 156).

Edwards' main treatise on the absolute sovereignty is his *Freedom of the Will* (1754).[1] The full title is illuminating: *A careful and strict Inquiry into the modern prevailing notions of that freedom of will which is supposed to be essential to moral agency, virtue and vice, reward and punishment, and praise and blame.* His position was that men's actions are voluntary, but not the less necessary. The necessity is moral because it concerns motives and volitions as distinguished from the natural necessity of the physical world. The moral quality of the choices men make is what they are accountable for, no matter what the causes that produced them.

For the proof both of the necessity and the accountability he relies both on Scripture and on reason. For him the issue at stake was a stark one. If we admit contingency and the

---

[1] Paul Ramsey (ed.), Yale University Press, 1959.

liberty of self-determination, then confidence both in the
existence of God and in the reality of his providence is shaken.
He was certainly right in this. The development of theology
has followed the direction he opposed with the consequences
he foresaw. But he is no help to us if we ask: accepting human
free-will, how do we affirm the reality of God, and the reality
of his providence?

Edwards was at one with the medieval thinkers in making
a distinction between what is self-existent, which is unchangeable in its eternity, and things that begin to be which
have the foundation of their existence outside themselves.
If things that are not in themselves necessary may begin to
be without a cause, the whole of our confidence about the
constitution of the world is taken away (pp. 181–2).

He is certain that the acts of the wills of moral agents are
not contingent events, because God has a certain fore-
knowledge of such events (p. 239). If this is not so, then the
predictions of Scripture are in fact not reliable, and God's
knowledge is inconsistent with itself (pp. 248, 260).

The consequences of this for the doctrine of providence
would be quite disastrous: 'It will also follow from this notion
that as God is liable to be continually repenting what he has
done, so he must be exposed to be constantly changing his
mind and intentions, as to his future conduct . . . For his
purposes, even as to the main parts of his Scheme, namely,
such as belong to the state of his moral kingdom, must
always be liable to be broken, through want of foresight; and
he must be continually putting his system to rights, as it
gets out of order, through the contingence of the actions of
moral agents . . . In such a situation, he must have little else
to do, but to mend broken links as well as he can, and be
rectifying his disjointed frame and disordered movements, in
the best manner the case will allow . . . It is in the power of
man, on these principles by his devices, purposes and actions,
thus to disappoint God, break his measures, make him continually to change his mind, subject him to vexation, and
bring him into confusion' (pp. 253–4).

Later theology can't blame Jonathan Edwards that it hasn't been warned.

(i) *The Appeal to Experience.* The emphasis on feeling and experience was as characteristic of the eighteenth century as its intellectualism. The most important influences here seem to be four.

[i] *Eighteenth-century Pietism.* The seventeenth century gave birth to Pietism. The eighteenth century saw its widespread development. But with the growth of influence there came an institutionalizing and a hardening. August Herrmann Francke (1663–1727) received the stimulating influence of the movement at the hands of P. J. Spener, and when the University of Halle was established in Halle in 1694 by the Elector of Brandenburg he made and kept it a centre of Pietism, until his death in 1727. He founded schools, he organized translations of spiritual classics, he corresponded far and wide till Pietism spread to England and North America, to Scandinavia, to south-east Europe and Russia and even to Central Asia. But in its spread Pietism hardened. It had no accession of leadership of the same quality after Francke's death. What had begun as a fresh discovery of Christianity as a living experience, turned into a painful struggle for repentance as the only method of fellowship with God. Yet it was a persistent influence towards the study of the Bible, lay responsibility and necessary endeavour.

A new impulse came from a movement which began in Pietism, but distinguished itself from it. The chief interest of Count Nikolaus Ludwig von Zinzendorf (1700–60) who was educated in one of Francke's educational institutions was evangelism. He welcomed on one of his estates Protestant emigrants from Austria, many of whom were descendants of the United Brethren of Bohemia. On 13th August 1727, in a vivid experience of love to Christ and love to one another, the Unity of the Moravian Brethren was reborn. While Pietism proper took its start from the experience of the individual

Christian, Zinzendorf and the Moravians found their basis in the Cross of Christ.

At a Synod in October 1740, under the chairmanship of Zinzendorf, the Moravians declared: 'The difference between those zealous servants of God, who in Germany by some were called Pietists, in England Methodists, in France Jansenists, in Italy and Spain Quietists, in the Roman Church in general often known by the character of preachers of repentance and ascetics, but in the Protestant Church generally thought Mystics, on the one side, and our Economy on the other, is this: the former strive either for an alteration in the religious worship; or are for abolishing all the External Part: We preach nothing but the Crucified Christ from the heart; and we think that when anyone gets hold of Him, all that is idle vanishes away from such a person, and all necessary good comes, together with the living and abiding impression of the loving and faithful Lamb of God, who was once a moral man in reality.'[1]

This intimate devotion to Jesus Christ as Saviour in the opinion of Zinzendorf and the Moravians was a Christianity of the heart which was greater than all the barriers of creed, forms of worship and ecclesiastical organization, and was the sufficient and satisfying ground on which Christians and Churches can all meet.

The contribution of Zinzendorf and the Moravians to Christian theology was first of all a form of the appeal to experience which stressed the given grace of Christ crucified: but in their concern for mission and Christian fellowship, they raise in contrasting ways the question of the nature of the Church.

Pietism thought of itself as an 'ecclesiola in ecclesia', an order within the Lutheran Church of Germany. Zinzendorf, though he thought of the different types of Churchmanship as *tropes* by which the unity of the spirit can be kept in spite of the diversity of creeds and liturgies, agreed with the

---

[1] *Acta Fratrum*, p. 83; quoted on pp. 71–2 of A. J. Lewis, *Zinzendorf*, S.C.M., 1962.

Pietists. He was deeply disappointed when the Moravian
Brethren felt that they must become a separate denomination. Both in the Pietists, and in Zinzendorf and the Moravians, are to be found a strong concern for Christian unity and
ecumenical fellowship. But the Pietists and Zinzendorf agreed
in seeing the unity as essentially undenominational to be realized here and now without any organic unity of the Church.

[ii] Jonathan Edwards made a noteworthy contribution to
the eighteenth-century appeal to experience in his *Religious
Affections* (1746). 'True religion in great part,' he asserted,
'consists in holy affections.'[1]

It is, however, important to understand that Edwards presupposed the apprehension of the truth of the Christian faith.
Indeed because he was fully aware of the mixture of good and
evil in the revival (the 'Great Awakening' 1740–3), the book
is his attempt to discriminate the authentic signs of the
presence of God and the Holy Spirit in the believer.

Affections are 'sensible' exercises of the inclination
expressed through the mind alone. The inclination in this is
called *heart*, but when it expresses itself in action it is called
will. The *heart* is not blind, but it is based on an apprehension
of the object to which it is responding. Love is in fact the
source of all other affections.

The sign to which Edwards attached the greatest importance, was the sign of consistent practice, for true
affections must show themselves in an outward and persistent
way. He based his treatise on I Peter 1, 1–8, and saw true
relationships as consisting in the affections of love and joy in
Christ—love depending on spiritual sight of the unseen
Christ, and joy being the result of faith.

On the negative side he insisted that the fact that affections
occur in a certain order is no certain indication that they are
evidence of the working of the Spirit; nor is the approval
of other certain evidence. 'The true saints have not such
a spirit of discerning, that they can certainly determine
who are godly, and who are not. For though they know

[1] Yale University Press, 1959, p. 95.

experimentally what true religion is, in the internal exercises of it; yet these are what they can neither feel, nor see
in the heart of another' (p. 181).

The main part of *Religious Affections* expounds twelve
signs of truly gracious and holy affections—signs being marks
through which we may discern the presence and working of
the divine Spirit. The first sign is that the affections must
arise from spiritual, supernatural and divine influences which
are inwardly perceived. The second and third signs make
clear that the affection must spring from response to the
beauty and sweetness of the moral excellency of divine things
in themselves and not from a sense of their benefit to ourselves. The fourth and fifth signs insist that the affections
must testify to the mind's enlightenment so that it under-
stands, and apprehends and is convinced by divine things.

True affections must, sixthly, be attended by evangelical
humiliation, not by legal humiliation. The one is that
humility which comes from a sense of the greatness of God,
the other comes from conscious renunciation of self. According to the seventh, eighth and ninth signs, they must exhibit
a remarkable and abiding change of nature, characterized by
the lamb-like, dove-like spirit and temper of Jesus Christ,
and a Christian tenderness of spirit.

The tenth sign is that beautiful symmetry and proportion
is to be seen in holy as opposed to false affections. They
create a spiritual appetite and longing after spiritual attain-
ments—the eleventh sign. Finally, and most importantly,
they must express themselves in sustained Christian practice
to the end of life. This is a testimony to the transformation
of the human heart by the divine spirit.

Edwards is fully aware of the fact of backsliding, and
considers carefully how far it may go. So he says, 'True
Saints may be guilty of some kinds and degrees of backsliding, and may be soiled by particular temptations, and may
fall into sin, yea great sins: but they can never fall away so,
as to grow weary of religion, and the service of God, and
habitually to dislike and neglect it' (p. 390).

In these twelve signs there is a recognition of the distinctively religious dimension of life. Within this dimension Edwards showed the understanding actively at work to clarify the experience of the individual. In this setting there are rational tests that can judge the genuineness or falsity of the emotions.

The question Edwards throws back on us is the one to which he himself gave a clear positive answer: how do we perceive the working of the divine?

[iii] A widely influential appeal to experience came from the complex teaching of Jean-Jacques Rousseau (1712–78). He combined an appeal to natural religion with a testimony to feeling as the uncriticizable basis of it all. His religious teaching is to be found in the *Profession of Faith of a Savoyard Priest* which is set out in the fourth book of his *Emile*[1] and in the final chapter on Civil Religion in his *Social Contract*.

He distinguished between three types of religion—the religion of man, the religion of the citizen, and the religion which acknowledges contradictory duties at the same time. The religion of the citizen is the acceptance of the dogmas, rites and external cult prescribed by law in a single country. The kind of religion which makes it impossible for people to be faithful both to religion and to citizenship he thought exemplified by the Lamas, and the Japanese and Roman Catholicism. The religion he really believed in was the religion of man 'which has neither temples, nor altars, nor rites, and is confined to the purely internal cult of the supreme God and the eternal obligations of morality, is the religion of the Gospel pure and simple, the true theism, what is called natural divine right or law'.[2]

The context of this religion is faith in God and acknowledgment of the moral law, and here Kant found an affinity with Rousseau. God conserves through justice the general order he has created through goodness. Conscience is an innate and indestructible tendency to choose the good.

[1] Everyman edn., pp. 228–58.
[2] *Social Contract*, Everyman edn., p. 117.

Rousseau apostrophizes 'Conscience! Conscience! Divine instrument, immortal voice from heaven; sure guide for a creature ignorant and finite indeed, yet intelligent and free; infallible judge of good and evil, making man like God! In thee consists the excellence of man's nature and the morality of his actions.'[1] However little borne out by his actions, this is an essential part of his thinking.

Though on this basis there is little place for Christianity, Rousseau was deeply indebted to its ideas of the Fall and Redemption. He used them for his own purposes and interpreted them as social maladjustment and a readjustment which is a possibility for evolving an enlightened man. But the basis of all this for Rousseau was feeling and this is the aspect of his thinking which has been so widely influential. 'To exist is to feel; our feeling is undoubtedly earlier than our intelligence, and we had feelings before we had ideas.' Here he notes: 'When we are chiefly concerned with the object and only think of ourselves as it were by reflection, that is an idea; when, on the other hand, the impression received excites our chief attention, and we only think in the second place of the object which caused it, it is a feeling.'[2]

'Let us listen to the inner voice of feeling; what healthy mind can reject its evidence?' Against those who deny that the visible order of the universe proclaims a supreme intelligence, Rousseau asked, 'How can you rob me of the spontaneous feeling which, in spite of myself, continually gives you the lie? I see God everywhere in his works; I feel him within myself.' On free-will Rousseau says: 'No material creature is in itself active. In vain do you argue this point with me; I feel it, and it is this feeling which speaks to me more forcibly than the reason which disputes it.' And Rousseau said to God: 'The best use I can make of my reason is to resign it before thee; my mind delights, my weakness rejoices, to feel myself overwhelmed by thy greatness.'[3]

Rousseau's influence has worked in two ways. It helped to

[1] *Emile*, p. 254.   [2] *Ibid.*, p. 253.
[3] *Ibid.*, pp. 237–9, 242, 249.

produce an emotional acceptance of Christian ideas even
where there was a respectful scepticism of their intellectual
content. On the other hand, it encouraged an emphasis on
an emotional religion of the individual, divorced from
historical and institutional Christianity, and not subject to
the criticisms of reason.

[iv] The appeal to experience to be found in John Wesley
(1703–91) has its own distinctive character. The originality
of John Wesley is the ability of an outstanding man of action
who welds material of a diverse kind provided by others into
his own type of unity, and alters the climate of opinion at
certain distinctive points. So his theology was fundamentally
traditional, and did not probe the foundations; but his
distinctive emphases are original and though controversial,
widely influential.

The foundations of his theology come from the Anglican
Reformers of the sixteenth century. This is to be seen in *The
Doctrine of Salvation, Faith and Good Works, extracted from
the Homilies of the Church of England* (1738). But he went
back to the Fathers to find his characteristic emphasis on
divine-human co-operation; he was steeped in the mysticism
of the Eastern Church and in the spirituality of à Kempis,
Pascal and Fénelon, and he borrowed an emphasis on the
assurance of faith from the Moravians. From these diverse
materials he built a consistent doctrine of salvation, which
was dark and sombre in its picture of human depravity and
helplessness and unlimitedly optimistic about man redeemed
and sanctified by Christ. It was this outlook he expected
people to find in the Bible if they would watch for 'the
connection and harmony there is between those grand
fundamental doctrines, original sin, justification by faith, the
new birth, inward and outward holiness'.[1]

In this context he resolutely took and popularized the anti-
Calvinistic stance, emphasizing the moral transformation of
the Christian rather than the absolute sovereignty of God.
While he believed and taught that righteousness is *imputed*

[1] *Works*, XIV, pp. 276–8.

to us when we are justified in faith, he was insistent that the aim of justification is that righteousness should also be *imparted* to us.

A characteristic statement of his anti-Calvinism is to be found in his *Predestination Calmly Considered*: 'I appeal to every impartial mind, whether the mercy of God would not be far less gloriously displayed in saving a few by his irre-sistible power, and leaving all the rest without help, without hope, to perish everlastingly, than in offering salvation to every creature, actually saving all that consent thereto and doing for the rest all that infinite wisdom, almighty power and boundless love can do without forcing them to be saved —which would be to destroy the very nature that he had given them.'[1] Wesley appeals to experience within an accepted framework of doctrine, which he believes is based on the revelation given in the Bible. He uses his reason in this and he will have no depreciation of it, but the scope he gives to it in assessing truth is limited. It is in experience that the truths of doctrine become certain possessions.

Wesley's position may be studied in his 'Earnest Appeal to Men of Reason and Religion' (1743). 'Christianity,' he said, 'is a religion of love and joy and peace, having its seat in the inmost soul but ever showing itself by its fruits, con-tinually springing forth not only in all innocence—for love worketh no ill to his neighbour—but likewise in every kind of beneficence, spreading virtue and happiness all around it.'[2]

'Faith is that divine evidence whereby the spiritual man discerneth God and the things of God. It is with regard to the spiritual world what sense is with regard to the natural. It is the spiritual sensation of every soul that is born of God . . . Faith, according to the scriptural account, is the eye of the new-born soul . . . It is the feeling of the soul whereby a believer perceives, through the "power of the highest over-shadowing him", both the existence and the presence of him

[1] Text in *John Wesley*, A. C. Outler (ed.), O.U.P., 1964, p. 452.
[2] Text in *op. cit.*, pp. 384–424.

in whom "he lives, moves and has his being", and indeed the whole invisible world, the entire system of things eternal. And hereby, in particular, he feels "the love of God shed abroad in his heart" . . . No man is able to work it, in himself. It is a work of omnipotence. It requires no less power thus to quicken a dead soul than to raise a body that lies in the grave. It is a new creation, and none can create a soul anew but he who at first created the heavens and the earth' (pp. 386–7).

Wesley insisted that faith is *reasonable*. If anyone 'departs from true, genuine reason, so far he departs from Christianity', and from the written word of Scripture. 'We join with you, then in desiring a religion founded on reason and every way agreeable thereto. But one question still remained to be asked: What do you mean by "reason"? I suppose you mean the eternal reason, or the nature of things: the nature of God and the nature of man, with the relations necessarily subsisting between them. Why this is the very reason *we* preach: a religion evidently founded on, and every way agreeable to, eternal reason, to the essential nature of things.'

'But perhaps by reason you mean the faculty of reasoning, of inferring one thing from another. There are many, it is confessed (particularly those who are styled "mystic divines"), that utterly decry the use of reason, thus understood in religion; nay that condemn all reasoning concerning the things of God as utterly destructive of true religion. But we can in no wise agree with this. We can find no authority for it in Holy Writ. So far from it we find there both our Lord and his Apostles continually reasoning with their opposers . . . We therefore not only allow but earnestly exhort all who seek after true religion to use all the reason which God hath given them in searching out the things of God. But your reasoning justly, not only on this but on any subject whatsoever, presupposes true judgments already formed whereon to ground your argumentation.'

But reason cannot judge Christian truth unless it rests on the insight of faith. In order to form a true judgment of the

things of God you need new spiritual senses—the hearing ear
and the seeing eye. 'And till you have these "internal senses"
till the eyes of your understanding are opened, you have no
apprehension of divine things, no idea of them at all. Nor
consequently, till then, can you either *judge truly*, or *reason
justly* concerning them, seeing your reason has no ground
whereon to stand, no materials to work upon' (pp. 394–5).

Faith Implies Assurance. Wesley asked: 'But perhaps you
doubt whether that faith whereby we are saved implies such
a trust and confidence in God as we describe.' Many condemn such assurance—some who want to be Christians, all
nominal Christians, and the Roman Catholic Church. Against
this Wesley appealed to the Homilies, and to the witness in
every man's breast. 'Whatever expressions any sinner who
loves God uses to denote God's love to him, you will always,
upon examination, find that they directly or indirectly imply
forgiveness. Pardoning love is still at the root of all . . . A
confidence then in a pardoning God is essential to saving
faith' (p. 406).

If we ask how Wesley acquired this confidence in a sensible
testimony to saving faith, the answer seems to be first in his
own experience on Wednesday, 24th May 1738, in Aldersgate
Street, as he heard Luther's 'Preface' to *The Epistle to the
Romans* when he felt his 'heart strangely warmed'. As he
said: 'I felt I did trust in Christ, in Christ alone for salvation;
and an assurance was given me that he had taken away *my*
sins, even *mine*, and saved me from the law of sin and death.'
This experience might not have been determinative if it had
not been confirmed by the success of his mission in April
1739. So he came to count as a proof that there is a direct
testimony of the Holy Spirit in the believing soul 'because
this plain meaning of the word of God is confirmed by the
experience of innumerable children of God'.[1] Though Wesley
came to admit that a man might be a Christian without the
feeling of assurance, he always thought that to have it was
normal for every Christian.

[1] *Works*, V, p. 132.

Faith Also Implies Perfection. Wesley's teaching on perfection is entirely of a piece with his other teaching. It came out of his conviction that, when God asks us to love with all our heart, mind, soul and strength, this is a reasonable request and we can set no limits to what his grace can do in a human heart. It also comes of his sense that in his ministry God is bringing his purposes to fulfilment. 'Behold the day of the Lord is come. He is again visiting and redeeming his people. Having eyes, see you not? Having ears, do you not hear, neither understand with your hearts? At this hour the Lord is rolling away our reproach. Already his standard is set up. His Spirit is poured forth as the outcasts of men and his love shed abroad in their hearts. Love of all mankind, meekness, gentlemen, humble of mind, holy and heavenly affections, do take place of hate, anger, pride, revenge, and vile or vain affections' (p. 423).

Just as there is a sensible token that we are justified, so there must be a sensible token that we are fully sanctified, that the love to God in our heart is entire and complete, even though imperfections still remain. God brings this about in the soul by a simple act of faith, in a moment, though there is a growth before and after. Wesley thinks that for the majority of believers the state of perfection was only reached in the hour of death, though he thought that some became perfect before death, and that there will be progress on the other side of death.

'What is faith whereby we are sanctified, saved from, and perfected in love?' Wesley asked. His answer was: 'It is a divine evidence and conviction, first, that God hath promised it in the Holy Scripture . . . It is a divine evidence and conviction, secondly, that what God hath promised, he is *able* to perform . . . It is, thirdly, a divine evidence and conviction that he is able and willing to do it now . . . To this confidence that God is both able and willing to sanctify us *now*, there needs to be added one thing more—a divine evidence and conviction that *he doth it* . . . But does God work this great work in the soul *gradually* or *instantaneously*? Perhaps it may be gradually wrought in some . . . but certainly you may look for it *now*, if you believe it is by faith' (pp. 281–2).

Wesley did not solve the intellectual problems connected with his appeal to experience, nor the relation of Christians to the sources of Christian faith. He handed them on to the subsequent century.

He also handed on the problem of the right doctrine of the Church. He himself maintained steadily that the Methodist Movement was simply an evangelical order within the Church Catholic.[1] But in two ways he helped the movement to become a denomination. His four Appeals on behalf of the movement to the Church of England met with no response, but they certainly strengthened the confidence of Methodists in their own corporate and independent witness. Also, when under the pressure of the practical situation he set apart Richard Whatcoat and Thomas Vasey as presbyters, and ordained Dr. Coke to the office of 'Superintendent of the Societies in America', he took a step which in the course of time made Methodism a denomination. But his doctrine of the Church remained that of his early years and did not take account of the result of his own remarkable work of evangelization.

[1] See Sermon XIV, 'On Attending the Church Service', *Works*, VII, 174–85.

III—THE NINETEENTH CENTURY

CHRISTIAN THEOLOGY IN THE PERSPECTIVE OF HISTORY

General Characteristics

The nineteenth century was a time of a great ferment of ideas which only revealed their full revolutionary significance in the twentieth century. It was the century in which the true nature and methods of historical study became understood, and in which there was a vast new investigation of historical material. The pervasive influence of a new understanding of change and the historical powers is felt throughout it. This meant a widening of the horizons of knowledge —in historical studies themselves in which Leopold van Ranke (1795–1886) is an outstanding name; in the comparative study of religion, in which F. Max Müller (1823–1900) did outstanding work in editing and translating texts, and in natural science, in which perhaps the most famous name is that of Charles Darwin (1809–82).

The new understanding of history meant also that the question of the truth of Christian theology was raised in a new way, and the nineteenth century bequeathed the problems unsolved to its successor. If all human life is to be seen within a historical perspective, in what way is it now possible to affirm God transcendent incarnate in Christ? What is the nature of the Church, and under what conditions does it give trustworthy knowledge of God? What is the relation between Christianity and other religions? Can the truth of religion be a unifying factor in the life of mankind?

1. *Orthodoxy*

In the nineteenth century the Orthodox Churches experienced a revival of nationalism, missions, spirituality and theology. In the Balkans where the countries won new freedom from Turkish rule the Churches were not ready to develop theology; but in Russia where there was a great increase in spiritual direction, out of which came new missionary activity, a new confidence in the distinctive mission of the Church, and of the Orthodox Churches as the transmitter of its true tradition, arose.

On the doctrine of the Church three names may be mentioned. Alexei Khomiakov (1804–60) stressed the organic nature of Orthodox Church tradition which bred holiness through freedom in the spirit at one with itself. He set this over against Roman Catholicism in which he found unity without freedom, and Protestantism in which he found freedom without unity. He used the term *sobornost* to describe their togetherness in freedom which is characteristic of true Catholicity. 'The Church is not authority: the Church is truth and life.' Khomiakov's conception was more sacramental than mystical. The Church is an actual communion not only in truth but also in grace. He sought to give the Orthodox Churches a new confidence in themselves and to bring back their teaching to the standard of the Fathers and to the experience of actual Church life.

Philaret Drozdov (1782–1867), Metropolitan of Moscow 1821–67, probably the greatest theologian of the Russian Church in the nineteenth century, agreed substantially with Khomiakov but had a more generous attitude to Christians outside Orthodoxy. In his *Conversation of a Seeker and a Believer concerning the truth of the Eastern Greco-Russian Church* (1832) he insisted that the visible Church is only the external appearance of the Church invisible which can only be grasped by faith. The Eastern Church can be said to be the only true Church in the sense that it has been faithful to the original deposit of faith. But even 'impure' Churches belong to the mystery of unity. In the *Longer Catechism of the Orthodox Catholic Eastern Church* (1839) he insisted that tradition is necessary even now 'as a guide to the right understanding of the sacraments, and the preservation of sacred rites and ceremonies in the purity of their original institution'.[1]

Vladimir Soloviev (1853–1900) regarded a new unity of Christendom as the central problem of Christian life and history. He was an enigmatic figure combining pantheistic and Gnostic ideas with his Christian thinking and with a marked tendency to apocalyptic. In the end he joined the Roman Catholic Church in 1896 in order to express his conviction that Eastern and Western Christianity are essentially one. His vision was of the unity of the whole Church combining the spiritual insight of the Orthodox, the authority of Rome and the intellectual honesty of Protestantism.[2]

These Orthodox thinkers did not solve the problem of the nature and trustworthiness of the Church but they ensured that Orthodoxy should be taken seriously in the continuing discussion.

A different aspect of Orthodox theology was emphasized by the novels of F. M. Dostoievsky (1821–81). Dostoievsky portrayed the depth of sin and misery and the heights of saintliness expressed in boundless compassion for suffering sinful man. Material progress will not change the essential condition of man. This can only happen through the redeeming grace of God in Christ which he can do nothing to appropriate. The Legend of the Grand Inquisitor in Dostoievsky's novel *The Brothers Karamazov* expresses the dichotomy in his thinking between man's need of redemption and his desire for material betterment. For a satisfactory theology the dilemma in Dostoievsky's thinking, with its distrust of reason and moral effort, must be overcome within a theology of grace.

[1] P. Schaff, *The Creeds of the Greek and Latin Churches*, 1878, p. 449.
[2] *Russia and the Universal Church*, 1889, E.T., 1948.

2. *Catholicism*

The problem with which the Catholic Church wrestled in the nineteenth century is one which is essential to Christian theology: how can the Church be at once true to its own distinctive character and alive and responsive to the life, the thought, the needs of the world? The debate was unfinished and is unfinished yet.

One of the early powerful factors in it is the work of Felicité de Lamennais (1782–1854)—a man attractive both in his person and in his writings. The determining factor in his stormy career was his concern for the regeneration of society. In the end, when Pope Gregory XVI repudiated him in two encyclicals—*Mirari Vos* (1832) and *Singulari Vos* (1834)— he left the Church to continue his work outside it for what to him was the most important thing in life. There were two elements in his vivid thinking, and three stages of his endeavour to secure his purposes. There are the two elements of *Ultramontanism*—the appeal to the Pope 'beyond the mountains' as the supreme authority in the Church, and the deliverer of both the Church and society from their distress; and of *Liberalism*—the acceptance of a new state of society within which men had a new opportunity to think and plan and act. These two elements are in tension in Catholicism all through the century.

Lamennais began by opposing the Revolution, but then realized the shoddy condition of the French monarchy, and decisively turned against royalism. He espoused the cause of liberty, and his mind was fertile in finding new ways in which that liberty could be expressed. Against the restrictions on liberty by the French monarchy he turned to the Papacy; looking towards it with a passionate hope that it would abandon its temporal power and give spiritual leadership and direction to the mission of the Church to society to establish a new order of society in which moral regeneration would be found and constitutional liberty flourish.

Lamennais was ahead of his time. Though Gregory XVI

had not the suppleness of mind to perceive the constructive elements in Lamennais' thinking, Lamennais cannot be said to have found the right balance for the Church and its mission to the world. In his last book before leaving the Church, *Words of a Believer* (1834), he turned away from the authority of the Church in the field of society and painted a picture of the ideal community in which production and consumption were to be balanced harmoniously.

Johann Adam Moehler (1796–1854) is an interesting figure, because he represents a Catholic mind responding to the intellectual and emotional forces of the time—not least the Romantic Movement and the theology of Schleiermacher—and trying to use them for the enrichment of Catholic thinking. In his early work *Unity in the Church* (1825) he built a doctrine of the Church on its inner unity in the Holy Spirit. Christian doctrine is the ideal expression of the Christian spirit. Christian knowledge becomes more exact and clear as the Church grows into the manhood of Christ. The Church is the external and visible manifestation of love inspired by the Holy Spirit. The unity of the whole episcopate corresponds to the inner spiritual unity of the faithful. After hesitating over the Primacy, Moehler in the end accepted it as the keystone in the arch in the building of the Church.

He soon came to see the weaknesses of this. In his *Symbolism: or Exposition of the Dogmatic Convictions of Catholics and Protestants according to their public Confessional Statements* (1832) he attacked the falsity of the foundation teaching of Protestantism, and portrays Catholicism as the permanent incarnation of the Son of God. In this he stresses the Incarnation of the Divine Word, and his entrusting his work to a visible society of men, having over them an authority originating in Christ and perpetuated in uninterrupted succession. Indeed the dogmatic decisions of the episcopate are infallible.

'The dogmatic decrees of the episcopate (united with the general head and centre) are infallible,' says Moehler, 'for it represents the Universal Church, and one doctrine of faith, falsely explained, would render the whole a prey to error. Hence, as the institution which Christ hath established for the preservation and the explanation of His doctrine, is subject in this its function to no error; so the organ, through which the Church speaks, is also exempt from error.'[1]

Moehler's work represents a serious attempt to grapple with the question of the nature of the Church rather than a convincing answer to the question of its trustworthiness.

The greatest Catholic thinker of the nineteenth century was *John Henry Newman* (1801–90). He brought into the Catholic Church not only his own genius but also his evangelical experience of God and his long and agonizing wrestling with the question whether the Church of England could be a trustworthy part of the Church Catholic. But when he joined the Roman Catholic Church he felt that he had come home, and it is as a Catholic thinker that he speaks to us. Newman's greatness came from his imaginative sensitiveness to the concrete forms of life, his acute awareness of the sceptical power of human reasoning, and his power of grappling in prose of great beauty with perennial questions.

In four fields especially he is continuingly influential.

(*a*) Newman probed the relation between faith and reason all through his life, expressing his essential position in his *University Sermons* (1834) and giving his fullest expression of it in *A Grammar of Assent* (1870). He started from the question, how do we justify the ordinary certitudes of life which have not come to us from logic and cannot be proved by it? He made a distinction between formal and informal inference. In informal inference, guided by the testimony of conscience, from a number of concurrent signs we proceed to a spontaneous conviction of the reality of God. The doing of this marks the transition from 'notional' to 'real' assent. This conviction, once reached, gives rise to other appropriate convictions, reached by an 'illative' or inferential sense.

This is the context in which Newman rightly asked about

the way in which we apprehend truth in natural and revealed religion. He stressed three factors. The first is the importance of obedience to conscience as the setting in which we can attain truth: the second is the importance of a sense of the antecedent probability in the gaining of conviction; finally, it is through the accumulation of converging probabilities that we come to definite assent. 'Real assents,' said Newman, 'are sometimes called beliefs, convictions, certitudes; and, as given to moral objects, they are perhaps as rare as they are powerful. Till we have them, in spite of a full apprehension and assent in the field of notions, we have no intellectual moorings, and are at the mercy of impulses, fancies, and wandering lights, whether as regards personal conduct, social and political action, or religion. These beliefs, be they true or false in the particular case, form the mind out of which they grow, and impart to it a seriousness and manliness which inspire in other minds a confidence in its views, and is one secret of persuasiveness and influence in the public stage of the world.'[1]

If we are to solve this problem today it will be along Newman's lines. The difficulty is the factor of antecedent probability. Readers of Newman may not be persuaded by *his* sense of the antecedent probability, and the Christian theologian today has the task of being faithful to his own sense of the antecedent probability in an age which denies it.

(*b*) Newman was deeply concerned with the problem of authority in religion. He rightly felt that religion is essentially obedience—the discovery of the great reality which claims our utter and complete devotion. He fell in love with the Church of the Fourth Century as he made clear in his *The Arians of the Fourth Century* (1833): and his further thought was determined by this. He dismissed popular Protestantism, which was all the Protestantism he knew, and wrote acutely of the difficulties involved in taking the Bible by itself without the interpretation of the Church as the final authority. This he set out in *The Prophetical Office of the Church* (1837)

---

[1] *Grammar of Assent*, Chapter IV, Section 2.

and in Tract 85, *Lectures on the Scripture Proof of the Doctrines of the Church* (1838).

But Newman was also concerned with the question whether the patristic age could be the final authority. He came to think, as he said in the 1878 edition of *The Prophetical Office of the Church*, that 'history and the patristical writings do not absolutely decide the truth or falsehood of all important theological propositions, any more than Scripture decides it'.[1] As we read the *Prophetical Office* in the light of what happened, it is easy to see that the criticisms of Romanism are not very convincing in the light of his interests, and that the attempt to find the infallible authority for the present through the Church simply out of the patristic period is not very satisfactory.

So Newman came to write his *Essay on the Development of Christian Doctrine* (1845) which took him finally into the Roman Catholic Church. This book has been widely influential in securing acknowledgment that there has been development. The distinctive features of Newman's discussion are twofold.

(i) Newman set as the first of seven pragmatic tests— fidelity to the original idea. He meant by idea a judgment which is firmly fixed in our minds and has a firm hold over our life. For the nature of the essential idea of the Church Newman turns to his beloved patristic age.

'The fifth century,' he said, 'acts as a comment on the obscure text of the centuries before it, and brings out a meaning, which with the help of the comment any candid person sees really to be theirs' (III. ii). When he looked at it the other way he said: 'Had St. Athanasius or St. Ambrose come suddenly to life, it cannot be doubted what communion they would mistake for their own' (III. i). His justification for his taking the patristic idea as the text of the idea was: 'It is sometimes said that the stream is clearest near the spring. Whatever use may fairly be made of this image,

---

[1] *Via Media*, I, p. xlvii.

it does not apply to the history of a philosophy or sect, which, on the contrary, is more equable, and purer, and stronger when its bed has become deep, and broad, and full' (I. i).

But this approach begs the most difficult question—the nature of the essential idea in Christianity—and there has more recently come widespread agreement that the essential idea of the Church must be found in Scripture before it is found in the developed Church.

(ii) Newman also held that 'in proportion to the probability of true developments of doctrine and practice in the Divine Scheme, is the probability also of the appointment in that scheme of an external authority to decide upon them . . . This is the doctrine of the infallibility of the Church.' And his reason for thinking this is because: 'the supremacy of conscience is the essence of natural religion: the supremacy of Apostle, or Pope, or Church or Bishop is the essence of revealed' (II. ii). Newman has not solved the problem of authority for Christian theology, but he has made clear the difficulties that must be met if it is thought right both to hold to God's special revelation but to deny that the infallible authority which governs Christians is an external objective authority.

(c) But Newman did not leave it there. What is the relation between the supremacy of conscience and the supremacy of the Pope? Newman, for the most part, was driven to publication by a concrete stimulus. Charles Kingsley in 1864 gave him the opportunity of vindicating his meticulous and agonising search for truth in his *Apologia pro vita sua;* Gladstone in 1874, by publishing a pamphlet on *The Vatican Decrees in their bearing on Civil Allegiance*, drove Newman to answer it in his *Letter to the Duke of Norfolk*, and to show that in many cases it is essential for a Christian to stand to his Christian convictions rather than accept a requirement of the State.

On the specific question of the Church and the individual conscience Newman began by insisting: 'We must either give

up the belief in the Church as a divine institution altogether,
or we must recognize it at this day in that communion of
which the Pope is the head.'[1] He said that if he was caught
in a conflict due to his double allegiance to Church and
State, he would decide 'according to the particular case,
which is beyond all rule, and must be decided on its merits'
(p. 243). He would consult the theologians, bishops and
clergy, and his friends, but if he could not take their view of
the matter he would rule himself by his own judgment and
his own conscience (p. 244). For 'did the Pope speak against
conscience in the true sense of the word, he would commit a
suicidal act. He would be cutting the ground from under his
feet. His very mission is to proclaim the moral law, and to
protect and strengthen that "Light which enlighteneth every
man that cometh into the world". On the law of conscience
and its sacredness are founded both his authority in theory
and his power in fact' (p. 252).

Newman insisted that he has not misrepresented Catholic
doctrine 'on the duty of obeying our conscience at all
hazards' (p. 259). And he added: 'Certainly, if I am obliged
to bring religion into after dinner toasts (which indeed does
not seem quite the thing), I shall drink—to the Pope, if you
please—still, to conscience first, and to the Pope afterwards'
(p. 261).

The question that Newman has bequeathed here to the
twentieth century is this: is the combination of the supremacy
of conscience and an infallible teaching authority a possible
one, or if the supremacy of conscience is maintained must not
the nature of the authority of the Church and its application
be understood differently from what it has been?

(d) Finally, Newman stressed the importance of the
independent cultivation of the mind and, in this connection,
the importance of the role of the laity in the Church. In the
lectures published as *The Idea of the University* (1852-9) he
discussed the place of theology in university education,
arguing that, if it were left out, other subjects would not be

---

[1] *Difficulties of Anglicans*, Vol. II (1907), p. 208.

seen in perspective, and that the cultivation of the intellect had an independent value of its own, not to be subordinated to religious principle. The situation in which Newman lived has gone. We have no such whole of knowledge as he presupposed nor any generally agreed 'liberal education'. But his open-minded treatment is a most illuminating background to the consideration of the same questions in a new day. With the *Idea of the University* may be linked Newman's article *On Consulting the Faithful in Matters of Doctrine* (1859) in which he vindicated from the patristic age the value of 'the consent of the faithful' as one of the ways of discovering what was actually revealed. In both of these spheres the independence of the Christian laity within its own sphere was emphasized.

The dominant figure in nineteenth-century Catholicism was undoubtedly Pope Pius IX (1792–1878). He saw his temporal power gradually decrease, and in 1870 he was deprived of all but a formal temporal power when Victor Emmanuel captured Rome. But during his reign as Pope, confidence in the Papacy increased in the Church, many new dioceses and missionary centres were established, and concordats with many European and American governments concluded.

He saw his work as protecting and affirming the distinctive character of the Church against the current of the life of the world. In 1854 he defined the dogma of the immaculate conception of the Blessed Virgin Mary. The dogma declared that Mary 'at the first instant of her conception was preserved immaculate from all stain of original sin, by the singular grace and privilege granted her by Almighty God, through the merits of Jesus Christ, Saviour of Mankind'.

In 1864 he condemned contemporary rationalism, pantheism and liberalism which conflicted with Catholic doctrine in the *Syllabus of Errors* attached to the Encyclical *Quanta Cura*. Among the errors repudiated were the idea 'that the liberty of conscience and of worship is the peculiar (or inalienable) right of every man', and the idea that 'the

Roman Pontiff can and ought to reconcile himself to, and agree with, progress, liberalism, and civilization, as lately introduced.'

In 1869–70 the first Vatican Council took place. Two Dogmatic constitutions were promulgated. *The Dogmatic Constitution on the Catholic Faith* began by affirming God the Creator of all things; and that God may be certainly known by the natural light of human reason, but it pleased God to reveal himself to mankind also by another supernatural way. Faith, the full obedience of our intelligence and will, is a response to the authority of God. There can never be any real discrepancy between faith or reason. And that meaning of the sacred dogmas is perpetually to be retained which our holy mother the Church has once declared.

The other dogmatic constitution was called *The First Dogmatic Constitution on the Church*. It dealt with 'the institution, perpetuity, and nature of the sacred Apostolic Primacy'. No other was promulgated because the Franco-Russian War put an end to the proceedings. The crucial passage is a moderately worded statement of the infallibility of the Pope: 'We teach and define that it is a dogma divinely revealed: that the Roman Pontiff, when he speaks *ex cathedra*, that is, when in discharge of the office of pastor and doctor of all Christians, by virtue of his supreme Apostolic authority, he defines a doctrine regarding faith or morals to be held by the Universal Church, by the divine assistance promised to him in blessed Peter, is possessed of that infallibility with which the divine Redeemer willed that his Church should be endowed for defining doctrine regarding faith or morals; and that therefore such definitions of the Roman Pontiff are irreformable of themselves, and not from the consent of the Church.'

It must be remembered that the theological activity of Pope Pius IX is one half of the question—the other being the responsiveness of the Church to the needs of the world—and that the discussion is continuing. Also that the carefully limited statement of Infallibility, in principle, raises no more

questions than does Newman's insistence that a special
Revelation implies an objective infallible authority.

The successor of Pope Pius IX, Pope Leo XIII (1810–1903,
Pope 1878–1903) was more diplomatic in his actions. Two
things are of great importance for Christian theology about
his reign. One is his encyclical *Aeterni Patris* (1879) in which
he commended to the Church the study of philosophy, and
especially the study of the works of St. Thomas Aquinas.
Where the claims of St. Thomas have not been thought
absolute the effect of this encyclical has been the widening of
intellectual horizons.

The other notable aspect of Pope Leo XIII's reign is the
stimulus his apparently liberal attitude—he opened the
Vatican archives to historical research and he encouraged
the study of the Bible in the Encyclical *Providentissimus
Deus* — gave to unorthodox thinking in a diverse group of
thinkers who came to be known as 'Modernists'. They adopted
whole-heartedly the critical view of the Bible, they were anti-
scholastic and in favour of pragmatic thinking and they found
the meaning of history in its outcome rather than in its origins.

The critical Biblical approach was represented by Alfred
Loisy (1857–1940) who eventually wrote *The Gospel and
Church* (1902) as a refutation of Adolf von Harnack's *What is
Christianity?* It was a vivid apologetic for Catholicism but it
gave up the traditional view of historical origins and the
Scholastic type of theology. It was promptly repudiated and
Loisy eventually (1908) left the Catholic Church to continue
as an independent Biblical critic.

The pragmatic theological approach was represented by
George Tyrrell (1861–1909), who affirmed the spirituality of
the Catholic Church in its Christ-centredness. He denied that
there could be an absolute or unchangeable statement of the
theology which is the intellectual formulation of that
spirituality. He stressed the immanence of God, and his
revelation through religious experience. He also was ex-
communicated.

Much of the thinking of the Modernists was unsatisfactory

as an adequate expression of Christian truth. Yet it was very harshly suppressed in 1907 by Pope St. Pius X (Pope 1903–14). and in 1910 an anti-Modernist oath was imposed on all clerics. But from about the last decade of the century Catholic thinkers generally became open to the impact of the intellectual forces round about them and this was a permanently enriching stimulus. And some elements in the Modernist thinking have reappeared in a new form in the thinking of the Second Vatican Council (1962–5).

3. *Christianity in Britain*

An important teacher of all types of Christian theologians in Britain in the nineteenth century was Samuel Taylor Coleridge (1772–1834). His mind was not systematic but penetrating; and he gave expression to seed thoughts for the future and that in three ways:

(i) *His Distinction between Reason and Understanding.* In making this distinction he was influenced by Kant, but Coleridge had greater confidence in the power of the mind to apprehend spiritual reality. *Understanding* is the term he uses for the activity of the mind in relation to sense-experience. But within the total activity of the mind there is not only understanding but reason. *Reason* is the source of truth above sense. In relation to abstract truth it is speculative reason, in relation to moral truth it is practical reason, in relation to revealed truth it is the spirit of the regenerated man. *Understanding* is concerned with quantities, qualities and relations of particulars in time and space. *Reason* is the distinctively human use of the mind, and enables men to respond to what is real with the whole of their being.[1] Coleridge was not the first to make the distinction, nor did he give a fully satisfying account of the nature of the richer use of the mind: but he gave the distinction, which is essential to Christian theology, a new currency.

[1] 'On difference in kind of reason and the understanding' in *Aids to Reflection* (1825).

(ii) *His Attitude to the Bible*. Coleridge's deepest conviction was of the utter reality of God as spiritually apprehended—the divine Lord, by whose Word and Spirit as the transcendent cause, whatever substantially exists, comes to be. And so he believes that there is a Light higher than all, of which light itself is only the tabernacle—'the Word that is light for every man, and life for as many as give heed to it'. So his principle was to read the Bible—'the written Letter'—to find evidence of that higher light. And he found in the Bible, as he says, 'words for my inmost thoughts, songs for my joy, utterances for my hidden griefs and pleadings for my shame and my feebleness. In short whatever *finds* me, bears witness for itself that it has proceeded from a Holy Spirit, even from the same Spirit which, remaining in itself, yet regenerateth other powers, and in all ages entering into holy souls, maketh them friends of God and prophets' (Wisdom 7.27).[1]

Or, as he said: 'the more tranquilly an inquirer takes up the Bible as he would any other body of ancient writings, the livelier and steadier will be his impressions of its superiority to all other books, till at length all other books and all other knowledge will be valuable in his eyes in proportion as they help him to a better understanding of his Bible. Difficulty after difficulty has been overcome from the time that I began to study the Scripture with a free and unboding spirit, under the conviction that my faith in the Incarnate Word and his Gospel was secure, whatever the result might be.'[2] The question remains whether the grounds of Coleridge's 'faith in the Incarnate Word and his Gospel' that he brought to the reading of the Bible are well based; but he certainly helped people to look to the central convictions of the Bible rather than to its more difficult utterances.

(iii) *His Emphasis on the Church*. Not all Coleridge's readers thanked him for the distinction he drew between the National Church and the Catholic Church in his book *On the*

[1] Letter I, *Confessions of an Inquiring Spirit*, published posthumously 1840.
[2] *Op. cit.*, Letter VI.

Constitution of Church and State (1830). The Church of
England *as the National Church* was a 'clerisy' that is, not
inherently Christian but an estate of the realm, necessary to
every nation for transmitting its cultural inheritance. The
Church of England *as the Catholic Church* was a 'blessed
accident'. By this he meant that 'Christianity is an aid and
instrument which no State or realm could have produced out
of its own elements' (1852 edn., pp. 65–6).

This emphasis on the Catholic Church as something other
than a creature of the State, that is, a divinely commissioned
spiritual society, with a distinctive character given by God,
was a spur to the rise of the Oxford Movement, and permanently valuable.

Of the Oxford Movement Newman was the fascinating
spearhead, but inevitably he left it for his true home in the
Roman Catholic Church: the abiding element in the Oxford
Movement was the earnest piety of John Keble (1792–1866)
and the devout scholarship of Edward Bouverie Pusey
(1806–82). What Newman gave to the Oxford Movement was
his inspiring leadership, his scriptural expositions in the
Parochial and Plain Sermons (1834–42) and his emphasis on
the urgency of holiness, not least in his lectures on *Justification* (1838). This latter is a moving testimony to the in-
dwelling of Christ in the human heart as the source of holiness. The controversial element in it is a minimizing of Faith
in relation to the Sacraments as means of grace.

The importance of the Oxford Movement lies not in its
meeting the needs of Christian theology but in its meeting the
needs of the worshipping heart. Its emphasis on the centrality
of worship and the need to make it worthy of the object of
worship has exercised a continuing beneficent influence.
This emphasis on the centrality of worship was set in the
context of the affirmation of the greatness of the patristic
tradition, the dignity of the calling of the Church, and the
urgency of practical holiness.

The Oxford Movement had its beneficial effects in spite of
its limitations as a clerical conservative movement. It was

not able intrinsically to give an intellectual lead to meet the
new stirrings in the century—the new understanding of
science, the new understanding of history, and the new
criticism of the Bible. It needed a new initiative in the third
generation to do this.

In the middle of the century Frederick Denison Maurice
(1805–72) was the most important thinker. The key to the
understanding of Maurice lies in two factors: 1—His sense
of the presence of God as a living Divine person, in his own
experience, which was his test of Christian truth. This was
why he was so incensed by H. L. Mansel (1820–71) who
argued in his Bampton Lectures that human reason was
unable to arrive at God, and so had to rely on the Revelation
contained in the Scriptures judged not on its contents but
received on the strength of the external evidences, particularly in the evidence of miracles. 2—His 'Platonic realism'
by which he believed in transcendental realities of which the
earthly embodiments were imperfect representations. It was
the realities in which he sought to persuade men to believe,
not their ephemeral embodiments.

On the basis of these two convictions he sought to present
the truth of the Scriptures and the faith of the Church.
Maurice's 'Platonic realism' was given a particular twist in
that for him there were certain absolute and unalterable
signs of the universal society for which the world longed, and
of which the Church is a foretaste. These were: Baptism, the
Creed—the Forms of Worship which have subsisted through
all the revolutions to which Christendom has been subjected
—the Eucharist, the Episcopate, the Scriptures. They are
signs of the universal society which God has founded. The
signs themselves, not any particular interpretation of them
which may be erroneous, ever and again recall us to the
enduring realities to which they testify. Neither sign nor
the reality it signifies can, in Maurice's judgment, ever be
questioned.

In his whole way of thinking Maurice sought to move the
reader away from religion to God, away from notions or

G

opinions and systems to realities, and away from sectarianism to what is universal. In this context Maurice asserted that Christ is the Head of mankind, and every man is in Christ whether he knows it or not. The foundation of Christian theology does not lie in sin, however deep its ravages. It lies in the fact that prior to sin mankind has been created in Christ who is the image of God.

Maurice knew that his *Theological Essays* (1853) would provoke a storm and so they did. He was right in calling attention to the present element in his final essay 'On Eternal Life and Eternal Death' which was found specially offensive, and to 'the entire surrender of the whole spirit and body' of Jesus on the Cross in which 'the true sinless root of Humanity' was revealed, in his essay on the Atonement. But the reigning Evangelical Orthodoxy was right in calling attention to the way he minimized the futurist and trans-actional expiatory elements in the Scriptures.

The twentieth century has been greatly stimulated by Maurice because of his emphasis on what he took to be the central elements of Christian conviction. But he did not solve the problem of why the particular things to which he called attention are realities and not opinions, as the objects of other men's judgments are. Maurice did not explain. He merely asserted, and he was annoyed if his main convictions were questioned.

His emphasis on Christ as the Head of mankind has a permanent validity. Yet the fact that men have been created in the image of God which is Christ, needs to be balanced by the fact that men have been redeemed by Christ, but have responded to the redemption only to a very limited extent.

And Maurice in his Platonic way bypassed the meaning of critical history. At times Maurice admitted that for knowledge of divine events we are dependent on human attestation, but asserted that, whatever the critics say, God will make himself known. At other times he insisted that whatever the Apostles Creed affirms must be accepted absolutely

as historic fact or there is no escape from atheism or pantheism. The real grappling with critical history lay ahead.

One sign of change came in Scotland from the publication
of *The Nature of the Atonement and its relation to remission of
sins and eternal life* in 1853 by John McLeod Campbell (1800–
72). He had been expelled from the ministry of the Church
of Scotland in 1831 for preaching that the universal Atonement of Christ is the only ground for assurance of God's love.
His book is a sustained repudiation of the penal doctrine of
the Atonement. His fundamental position he put clearly in a
question: 'The sufferings of Christ in making His soul an
offering for sin being what they were, was it the pain as pain,
and as a penal infliction?'; or was it, as Campbell held, 'the
pain as a condition and form of holiness and love under the
pressure of our sin and its consequent misery, that is presented to our faith as the essence of the sacrifice and its
atoning virtue?'[1] The Incarnate Son, in his death on the
Cross, is not punished by the Father for the sin of mankind;
he is one with the Father in holiness and love, he shares in the
Father's condemnation of sin, and he offers himself to the
Father as the way in which men may come to share God's
gift of eternal life.

He took his starting-point from Jonathan Edwards'
alternative in his *Satisfaction for Sin* (II. 1–3) that the
Mediator must either endure for sinners an equivalent
punishment, or offer to God for them an adequate sorrow and
repentance. This led him astray. For in addition to saying
that Christ expressed a perfect Amen in humanity to the
divine love in its yearnings over sinners (p. 127), Campbell
felt compelled to say that Christ expressed a perfect confession of our sins. Here he laid himself open to legitimate
criticism. For in saying that the response 'has all the
elements of a perfect repentance in humanity for all the sin
of man—a perfect sorrow—a perfect contrition—all the
elements of such a repentance, and that in absolute perfection
all—excepting the personal consciousness of sin', he expressed

[1] Sixth edn., 1886, p. 102.

a contradiction in terms. But his fundamental thought still stands, especially as the retrospective condemnation of sin is essential to the prospective divine purpose to make us in Christ partakers in eternal life.

The French Revolution had the effect of driving British theology in upon itself and isolating it from the development of Biblical criticism on the continent of Europe. So it was that a volume of *Essays and Reviews* published in 1860 burst like a bombshell and created an uproar. The central emphasis of the book is, as Benjamin Jowett (1819–93) said in his Essay *On the Interpretation of Holy Scripture*: 'the time has come when it is no longer possible to ignore the results of criticism'. It also gave initial suggestions about how theology might be altered when Biblical criticism had been taken into account. Jowett's message was 'Interpret the Scripture like any other book'. There are many respects in which Scripture is unlike any other book; these will appear in the results of such an interpretation. The first step is to know the meaning, and this can only be done 'in the same careful and impartial way that we ascertain the meaning of Sophocles or of Plato'. This plea has been universally accepted in responsible study of Christian theology.

The one essay which did not fit in to the general pattern was that by Mark Pattison (1813–84) on *Tendencies of Religious Thought in England 1688–1750*. This was a permanently valid plea that the study of the history of Christian theology is an essential tool for the study of contemporary questions. He thought that an examination of the faults of the eighteenth century which had much good sense but not much else should help, at a time when the formulae of past thinking were dominant, to promote an examination of the basis on which Revelation is supposed to rest.

A more far-reaching education in the essential part Biblical criticism must play from now on in Christian theology came through the trial and condemnation of William Robertson Smith (1846–94) by the Free Church of Scotland for his articles on the Old Testament in a new edition of the *Encyclo-*

paedia Britannica begun in 1875. The matter was discussed
from 1876 to 1881. In the upshot Smith was condemned, but
the right of scholars to critical freedom was won. In his
explanatory lectures on *The Old Testament and the Jewish
Church* (1881) Smith made it plain that the problems the
critics had to solve were not invented by anti-supernaturalist
bias, and that he himself found no difficulty in holding
together the fact of 'God Himself speaking words of love and
life to the soul', 'the Holy Spirit still bearing witness in and
with the Word', and the fact that 'the Word to which this
spiritual testimony applies is a written word, which has a
history, which has to be read and explained like other ancient
books' (p. 4).

An important new step came from the publication in 1889,
by seven English High Churchmen who had been meeting
together for twelve years, of *Lux Mundi: A Series of Studies
in the Religion of the Incarnation*. The Editor was Charles
Gore (1853–1932), then the first Principal of Pusey House,
Oxford. The positive and important character of the new
step, and its limitation, comes out quite clearly in Gore's
preface. 'It is,' he said, 'an attempt to put the Catholic
faith into its right relation to modern intellectual effort.'
This is a new step away from the old Tractarian position. The
Church while 'standing firm in her old truths' is able 'to
welcome and give its place to all new knowledge'. The
authors aim only 'at interpreting the faith we have received'.
On the other hand, they are concerned that they live in an
epoch 'of profound transformation', 'and certain therefore
(1) to involve great changes in the *outlying departments of
theology* (italics not in original) where it is linked on to other
sciences; and (2) to necessitate some general re-statement of
its claim and meaning'. So it was a most valuable use in the
service of traditional Christian truth of the new ways of
thinking at the point they had then reached. It was not,
what is now necessary, a new affirmation of the Christian
faith as true from within the context of the new questioning.

What the essayists did was in the first place to reaffirm

Christian doctrine making use of the new teaching on evolution and development, especially in the essays on *The Christian Doctrine of God* by Aubrey Moore (1848–90) and on *The Incarnation in relation to Development* by J. R. Illingworth (1848–1915). In this Illingworth went too far in accepting the progress of secular civilization as necessarily in harmony with the Incarnation. In keeping with the whole trend of the book was the essay by Arthur Lyttleton which insisted that the truth of the Atonement must not be isolated from other parts of Christian doctrine.

The second notable emphasis in *Lux Mundi* was the acceptance of Biblical criticism especially as relating to the Old Testament. They took for granted that the New Testament was substantially historical, and did not have occasion to face the questions which the further development of criticism would raise. But in addition, Gore in a sustained study of the doctrine of the Holy Spirit, in which he dwelt on the gradualness of his operations in the Church and the world, came at last to the question of the Holy Spirit and Inspiration which formed the essay's title. Here he asked whether Jesus' use of the Old Testament determines literary and historical questions, and answered no. Jesus' use of Jonah's resurrection as a type of his own does not depend in any real degree on whether it is historical fact or allegory. He argued with the Pharisees on the assumption that David was the author of Psalm 110, but this does not determine the historical question. Acceptance of critical views on the interpretation of the Bible would not diminish reverence for it. The limitation of knowledge in Jesus which Gore's views implied he ascribed in a footnote to 'God's condescension' whereby he 'beggared himself' of divine prerogatives, to 'put himself in our place'. He developed this 'kenotic' view of the Incarnation in his Bampton Lectures on *The Incarnation of the Son of God* (1891) and in his *Dissertations on subjects connected with the Incarnation* (1895), convinced that he was making up for the inadequacy at this point of much patristic theology. But the debate continues.

At the opposite end of the theological spectrum to the *Lux Mundi* school is the thinking of the Unitarian divine, James Martineau (1805–1900). Martineau, like Newman, was concerned with the problem of authority. But whereas Newman, faced with the problem of finding an absolute authority, turned to find it in the Church, Martineau, faced with the same problem, put all his trust in the individual's awareness of the moral authority of God, and found in Jesus Christ the supreme exemplar of true communion between man and God.

Martineau put his position succinctly at the end of his study of *The Seat of Authority in Religion* (1890): 'As I look back on the foregoing discussions, a conclusion is forced upon me on which I cannot dwell without pain and dismay: viz. that Christianity, as defined and understood in all the Churches which formulated it, has been mainly evolved from what is transient and perishable in its sources: from what is unhistorical in its traditions, mythological in its preconceptions and misapprehended in the oracles of its prophets. From the fable of Eden to the imagination of the Last Trumpet, the whole story of the Divine Order of the world is dislocated and deformed.'[1]

In contrast to this trenchant exposition of the untrustworthiness of the Church Martineau set the religion of Jesus. So he says 'in turning to the historical residue from these inquiries, I am brought to a further conclusion in which I rest with peace and hope: viz. that Christianity, understood as the personal religion of Jesus Christ, stands clear of all the perishable elements, and realizes the true relation between man and God'.

Martineau's absolute separation between the Church and Jesus Christ has been called in question by further Biblical criticism, as well as by further study of the history of Christian theology. So too there has been criticism of the foundation of his theology—an argument from the creation to a Creator, and an emphasis on obligation as the fundamental ethical fact and on the reverence that is to be given to moral

[1] Fifth edn., pp. 716–19.

authority. He did not solve the problems for the next century.

4. *Christianity in America*

The American Christian theology of the nineteenth century was derivative in essence, though working out its borrowings in a new environment. Essentially it was an unresolved struggle between liberal and conservative. The liberal thinkers may be represented by William Ellery Channing (1780–1842), Horace Bushnell (1802–76) and Ralph Waldo Emerson (1803–82); and the conservative thinkers included Charles Hodge (1797–1878), John Williamson Nevin (1803–86), Carl Walther (1811–87) and Charles Krauth (1823–83).

Channing was minister of the Federal Street Church in Boston and became Unitarian though he disclaimed the title. His most notable utterance was his sermon at the Ordination of the Rev. Jared Sparks, Baltimore, 1819. His distinctive emphasis was to stress the rationality of the right interpretation of Scripture, the benevolence of the moral perfection of God, and the moral nature of man.

Scripture doctrine, he asserted, is to be accepted without reserve. But this applies chiefly to the New Testament, for the dispensation of Moses is adapted to the childhood of the human race. And its meaning is to be sought in the same manner as that of other books. Revelation is addressed to us as rational beings. With Jesus, we worship the Father as the one living and true God. Channing objected to the doctrine of the Trinity. Jesus is one mind, one soul, one being as truly as we are and equally distinct from the one God.

God, he thought, is morally perfect. His justice is the justice of a good being acting in harmony with perfect benevolence. The doctrine of total depravity is an outrage against the moral perfection of God. Christ was sent by the Father to effect a moral or spiritual deliverance of mankind: that is, to rescue men from sin and its consequence, and to bring them to a state of everlasting purity and happiness. This he did by his teachings, his promises of pardon, the light he has thrown on the path of duty, his example, his threatenings against incorrigible guilt, his discoveries of immorality, his sufferings and death, that signal event the Resurrection, his continual intercession, and the power with which he is invested of raising the dead, judging the world and conferring the everlasting rewards promised to the faithful.

All virtue, Channing insisted, has its foundation in the moral value of man, and in the power of forming his temper and life according to conscience. In this setting Channing advocated the duty of charitable judgment, especially towards those who differ from us in religious opinion.

Channing's influence was very great. He is of importance here as an early witness to the need for interpreting the Bible like any other book, and as a perpetual reminder that a satisfactory doctrine of sin must not minimize the moral responsibility of man.

Horace Bushnell grappled manfully with the problems of conservative theology, and that especially in his discussion of three questions:

(a) *The Language of theology.* In his 'Preliminary Dissertation of the Nature of Language as Related to Thought and Spirit' in *God in Christ* (1849)[1] he insisted that the terms used in theological thinking are 'never exact' (p. 89). Dogmatic propositions only give us 'the seeing of the authors at the precise standpoint occupied by them, at the time, and they are true only as seen from that point—and never even there, save in a proximate sense' (p. 99). To some extent words of thought are not only inexact but false as attributing form to that which really is out of form (p. 92). Indeed paradoxical statements are nearest to a well-rounded view of truth (p. 93). Behind these views was the theory that 'words of thought and spirit are possible in language only in virtue of the fact that there are forms provided in the world of sense, which are cognate to the mind, and fitted, by reason

[1] Text in *Horace Bushnell*, H. Shelton Smith (ed.), *A Library of Protestant Thought*, Oxford University Press, 1965.

of some hidden analogy, to represent or express its interior sentiments and thoughts' (p. 88). This is not a solution of the problems, but it is an interesting opening up of the discussion.

(*b*) *Christian nurture*, in his *Discourses on Christian Nurture* (1847) expanded in *Christian Nurture* (1861).[1] Here against current revivalism and individualism Bushnell insists that 'it is the only true idea of Christian education, that the child is to grow up in the life of a parent, and be a Christian, in principle, from his earliest years'. (p. 391). This is not a balanced statement of the Christian life, but it is a valuable emphasis on one aspect.

(*c*) *The Atonement* in *The Vicarious Sacrifice* (1886), with Parts III and IV modified by *Forgiveness and Law* (1874). Bushnell's main thought is that God himself suffered to redeem us. What he is against is the traditional theory that the divine nature did not suffer in Christ. He rightly saw that the whole question of the Incarnation is 'whether it is possible for the divine nature to be manifested in humanity.'[2] Christ built into his character the moral suffering of God in his compassion for guilty men. 'The bearing of our sins does mean that Christ bore them on his feeling'[3] (p. 282). In *Forgiveness and Law* he modified his thought within its main direction, by admitting the idea of self-propitiation within the suffering of God, as a necessary element in forgiveness, This is the overcoming of 'the sense of being hurt by wrong, indignations against wrong done to others, disgusts at what is loathsome, contempt of lies, hatred of oppression, anger hot against cruel inhumanities' (p. 315) in any willingness to forgive. What we have in Christ is no less than 'a self-propitiation of God' (p. 326). Bushnell's thought in this, as in all he wrote, is essentially a transitional theology.

In Ralph Waldo Emerson, for all his literary excellence, the liberal constructive effort in Christian theology has petered out into a nebulous transcendentalism with the main thrust of his thinking being an appeal to disciplined moral effort.

---

[1] Text in *op. cit.*   [2] *God in Christ* in *op. cit.*, p. 178.
[3] *The Vicarious Sacrifice* in *op. cit.*, p. 309.

The recall to the inheritance of classical theology came especially in three ways:

(i) In John Williamson Nevin (1803–86) and the Mercersburg Movement.[1] This was an isolated attempt in the small German Reformed Seminary in Mercersburg, Pennsylvania, to recall American Christian thinkers to the classical theology of the Reformation, and to a high doctrine of the Church and the Eucharist. With his colleague Philip Schaff (1819–93) Nevin fostered an historical understanding of Christian theology, expounded the Catholicity of Protestantism and found in Calvin's teaching an authoritative exposition of the Real Presence of Christ in the Eucharist.

(ii) In *Charles Krauth* (1823–83) in the East, and *Carl Walther* (1811–87) in the West recalling American Lutherans to the greatness of their heritage. Krauth stressed the Confessional Lutheran heritage.[2] Walther stressed the sole activity of God in salvation, and the power of His Word in ordering Church life (see his *The Proper Distinction between Law and Gospel*).[3]

(iii) In *Charles Hodge* (1797–1878) who represents an orderly, comprehensive and lucid exposition of Christian theology on an inerrant Biblical basis and in fidelity to the Reformed Confessions. (See his *Systematic Theology* in three volumes 1871–3.) Hodge reacted against the Biblical criticism he found in Germany during his student days, but within his chosen Biblical and Confessional basis, he was liberal. He recognized the human element in the composition of the Bible, and emphasized what the Bible actually teaches —not what its authors may have believed authoritative. He acknowledged Biblical truth wherever he found it, and he was generous in his understanding of the boundaries of salvation.

---

[1] Some texts in *The Mercersburg Theology*, James Hastings Nichols (ed.), *A Library of Protestant Thought*, Oxford University Press, 1966.

[2] See his *The Conservative Reformation and its Theology* (1871) reprinted by Augsburg Publishing House, Minneapolis, 1963.

[3] Trans. W. H. T. Dan, St. Louis Concordia Publishing House, 1929.

5. *The Main Protestant Debate*

(a) *A Revolution in Theological Starting-point, Method and Context.* Friedrich Daniel Ernst Schleiermacher (1768–1834), began a new period in Christian theology by the originality of his starting-point, the simplicity of his constructive plan, and the brilliance of his translation of traditional theological statements into conformity with his starting-point. He confronts us with a decision as to whether his starting-point is satisfactory:

(i) *His Starting-point.* That starting-point is an understanding of the nature of religion. He stated it to begin with in his early work: *Religion, Speeches to its cultured despisers* (1799). Here the second and fifth speech are most important. But he recapitulated it in his more mature and constructive work, *The Christian Faith according to the principles of the Protestant Church, set out in an organized form* (1821–3), in § 4.

Schleiermacher's fundamental idea is exceedingly obscure, but apparently it is the presence of the Infinite in our essential being in a way that transcends the distinction between subject and object. The essence of piety is that particular type of feeling which is the consciousness of being absolutely or unconditionally dependent.

If we turn first to Schleiermacher's mature expression of his theory in *The Christian Faith* we find that 'absolute dependence' means that it cannot arise from an object which is *given* to us because we could always react to it if it were, yet it is a sense 'that the whole of our spontaneous activity comes from a source outside of us'.

In his proposition which sums up his thesis he asserted that the consciousness of being absolutely dependent is the same as being in relation to God. But when we examine this, we find that the feeling of dependence is not conditioned by any previous knowledge of God; that the idea which the term 'God' implies is simply the most direct reflection of the feeling

of absolute dependence; that it signifies essentially the co-
determinant in this feeling, and that the feeling 'becomes a
clear self-consciousness only as this idea comes simultaneously
into being'. Schleiermacher said that 'the whence of our
receptive and active existence is to be designated by the
word "God", but he wanted it to be clearly understood that
the "possibility of God being in any way *given* is entirely
excluded".'

Schleiermacher rightly wanted to vindicate religion over
against intellectualism and rationalism. His confusion came
from taking dependence as the *central* religious experience
and excluding from it any reaction to that on which we are
dependent. Confusion is also inevitably involved in any
attempt to get beyond the distinction between subject and
object.

In an interesting passage in § 30 of *The Christian Faith*[1]
Schleiermacher insisted that doctrinal propositions are
primarily descriptions of human states, and that conceptions
of divine attributes and modes of action, and statements on
the constitution of the world, are only permissible if they
can be developed out of propositions of the first form. The
revolutionary character of his thinking would have been
clearer if he had limited himself to the first form.

The roots of all Schleiermacher's later thinking are to be
found in the *Speeches*. In the *Second Speech* on 'The Nature
of Religion' he said:[2] 'Piety cannot be an instinct craving for
a mess of metaphysical and ethical crumbs' (p. 31). 'It
resigns, at once, any claims on anything that belongs either
to science or morality' (p. 35). 'In itself it is an affection,
a revelation of the Infinite in the finite, God being seen in
it and it in God' (p. 36). 'Piety appears as a surrender, a
submission to be moved by the whole that stands over
against man' (p. 37). 'It is immediate, raised above all error
and misunderstanding. You lie directly on the bosom of the
infinite world' (p. 43). 'Your feeling is piety, in so far as it

---

[1] E.T., T. and T. Clark, 1928, pp. 125–7.
[2] Harper Torchbooks, New York, 1958.

expresses, in the manner described, the being and life common to you and to the All' (p. 45). 'Doctrines are not necessarily for religion itself, but reflection requires and creates them' (p. 87). 'Seeing then that I have presented nothing but just this immediate and original existence of God in us through feeling, how can anyone say that I have depicted a religion without God?' (p. 94).

In the *Fifth Speech* on 'The Religions' Schleiermacher asked us to 'discover religion in the religions' (p. 211), and not in any 'natural religion' (p. 231). While he held that 'the existing forms should not in themselves hinder any man from "constructing a religion of [his] own" ' (p. 24), yet he thinks that 'Christianity most and best is conscious of God, and of the divine order in religion and history' (p. 242).

'Judaism is long since dead' (p. 238). Its strictly religious element is nothing but 'a relation of universal immediate retribution' (p. 239). The whole idea of the religion is in the highest degree childlike (p. 240). But Christianity is 'just the intuition of the Universal resistance of finite things to the unity of the Whole, and of the way the Deity treats this resistance' (p. 241).

The importance of Christ, 'who has been the author of the noblest that there has yet been in religion', lies not in 'the purity of his moral teaching', nor 'the individuality of his character'. 'The truly divine element is the glorious clearness to which the great idea he came to exhibit attained in his soul' (p. 246). All this shows the determining centrality for Schleiermacher of the conception of religion as 'absolute dependence'.

(ii) *His Method.* Because Schleiermacher was working with a subjective method, what he expounded in *The Christian Faith* are not isolated items, but everything is held together in the unity of subjective experience.

Not only is that so, but he worked out his Doctrine of Faith in a flexible structure of astonishing simplicity. It has two parts: first, the religious self-consciousness both pre-supposed by and contained in every Christian religious

affection; second, the modification of this produced first by
sin and then by grace. Within each part and sub-part he
stated the religious self-consciousness and then related it to
God and also to the world.

He begins by finding in the religious self-consciousness a
relation between the world and God—the dependence of the
totality of finite being upon the Infinite; and then finds
divine attributes and the conditions of the world appropriate
to this.

The doctrine of sin falls easily into the pattern. Schleiermacher expounds sins as a state of man, the constitution of
the world in relation to sin, and the divine attributes which
relate to the consciousness of sin.

In his doctrine of grace Schleiermacher starts with the
state of the Christian as conscious of divine grace. The
constitution of the world through redemption provides
opportunity for the doctrine of the Church, because, according to Schleiermacher, all that comes to exist in the world
through redemption is embraced in the fellowship of believers.
All that is required to complete the structure is a statement
of the divine attributes which relate to redemption.

This method is an immense stimulus to unity, coherence
and simplicity of structure in Christian theology.

(iii) *His Content.* Schleiermacher's 'positivistic' conception
of dogmatic theology—that it is 'the Science which syste-
matizes the doctrine prevalent in a Christian Church at a
given time' (§ 19) has often been criticized, but it expresses
exactly what he himself did. In one sense his theology is
simply the Protestant theology of his own time. It is Christ-
centred and evangelical, in making central the overcoming of
sin by the grace of God in Jesus Christ. So he defined
Christianity in its peculiar essence as 'a monotheistic faith,
belonging to the teleological type of religion, and is essentially
distinguished from other such faiths by the fact that in it
everything is related to the redemption accomplished by
Jesus of Nazareth' (§ 11). The revolutionary character of his
dealing with the content of Christian truth came from

two factors: he translated the current theology into the idiom of 'absolute dependence', and he left out anything not amenable to this treatment as irrelevant to the religious consciousness.

So he has given his own sense to natural and supernatural factors in Christ (§ 13) and bent the classical Christological discussions to his purpose (§ 22). His doctrines of God, sin and grace are understandable when they are considered from his starting-point. His new interpretation of the Incarnation is that the constant power of Christ's God-consciousness was 'a veritable existence of God in him' (§ 94). His new interpretation of the Atonement is that, through sympathy (§ 104), Christ communicates to believers the power of his God-consciousness (§ 100), and accepts them into the fellowship of his unclouded blessedness (§ 101). The Church is constituted through the coming together of regenerate individuals to form a system of mutual interaction and co-operation (§ 115). 'The expression "Holy Spirit" must be understood to mean "the vital unity of the Christian fellowship as a moral personality" ' (§ 116).

Throughout he worked it out with a brilliance of craftsmanship which is beyond praise. Many of his conceptions have been widely influential. But whether they are justified depends wholly on the satisfactoriness of his starting-point.

(b) *A Revolution in the Method and Scope of Thinking: the Synthesis of Absolute and Finite Spirit.*

As with Kant, the importance of Hegel for Christian theology lies in the scope of his thinking as a whole. As a Lutheran, he had no use for a piety which did not think out its own implications. His fundamental theological theme was the relation of God to the universe, in which he made use of the theological concepts of Reconciliation, the Trinity and Jesus Christ as the union of God and man. But he also taught historians to look for reasons in history and to take seriously the fact of development, and he illuminated the nature of the corporate aspect of ethical action. Whereas Schleiermacher's central conception was the presence of God in the feeling of absolute dependence, Hegel's was the presence of Absolute Spirit in the thinking of finite spirit.

Hegel's works are threefold:

(i) *His Early Theological Writings.* These were not published until 1907. They show the transition in his thinking from a moralistic interpretation of Christianity heavily dependent upon Kant, to his own distinctive approach to and interpretation of Christianity as the overcoming of the alienation of the world by love.

(ii) A sketch of the whole philosophy to be worked out— *The Phenomenology of Spirit* (1802).

(iii) The total philosophy not completely worked out, but with the context clearly indicated either in summary form in *The Encyclopaedia of the Social Sciences* (1817) or in an extensive but unrevised form in the posthumously published lectures. In this we have:

(1) *The Logic* (1812–16). This sets out the metaphysical categories which the successive phases of man's interpretation of absolute truth take. (These are given in summary form in Part I of *The Encyclopaedia*.)

(2) *The Philosophy of Nature*—the detailed application of the categories in terms of Nature. This is given in Part II of *The Encyclopaedia*, but never in extended form.

(3) *The Philosophy of Spirit.* Of this, Hegel's *Philosophy of Law* (Recht) was published in 1821. The whole scope of it was given in summary form in Part III of *The Encyclopaedia*; and in more extended form in the posthumously published lectures on the philosophy of religion, on history of philosophy, on aesthetics, and on the philosophy of history.

The Philosophy of Spirit 'begins with the emergence of man from Nature and covers his development—or the development of spirit in him—from consciousness to self-consciousness. It is, roughly speaking, an ascent through psychological levels to ethics, world history, art, religion and

H

finally to "philosophy"—not as the exposition of any new context but as the full self-consciousness in which the philosophy of spirit culminates.'[1]

Hegel bequeathed to the world a dialectic—the movement of being, discovered by thought, from a thesis to its antithesis and the 'contradiction' resolved in a synthesis. This is at once something that happens in all phases of the universe and in the universe as a whole. His total philosophy, as a whole, is an example of it. Spirit, in contrast to its original unformed state, becomes alienated from itself in unthinking Nature, and finds itself again in the synthesis of Nature and Spirit. In this synthesis, in which the alienation is overcome and Spirit is reconciled to itself, are to be found the subjective Spirit (man's inner life), the objective Spirit (family, society, State) and the absolute Spirit (art, religion, philosophy).

Hegel's dialectic insists that the universe exhibits different levels of existence from inorganic matter to life, mind and spirit. At each stage the higher includes the lower. In Hegel's hands the dialectic is a sensitive instrument and not a mechanical process. His stress on the antitheses within the development of the universe enables Hegel to do a considerable measure of justice to the harsh areas of life with all their pain, frustration and oppression. Hegel's whole endeavour is a gigantic act of faith. 'The real is rational': it makes sense, though you would not at first sight think so; and 'the rational is the real'—our deepest insight into what ought to be is, in spite of all appearances, what Absolute Spirit in the universe is actually bringing about. So also his phrase 'World History is World Judgment' is a long-term act of faith in the manifestation of Absolute Spirit within the universe.

One of the great achievements of Hegel is his unfolding of the ethical demands and achievement of the corporate life of man. Here he consciously dissents from the abstractness of Kant's individualism, seeing the corporate life of man both as the context of individual moral decisions, and also as having a higher ethical importance. He makes a distinction

[1] G. R. G. Mure, *The Philosophy of Hegel*, O.U.P., 1965, p. 39.

between 'legality', which is the lowest level of ethical action; 'morality', the next highest level, is private individual morality; and 'corporate ethical standards' (*Sittlichkeit*) which is higher still. In this last the abstract subjective freedom of the individual articulates and makes good in the actual life of society its vague ideal of what ought to be. It is here that the lives of men are shaped. Hegel insisted that the State must respect particular rights and duties which subserve its well-being, because Society is an essential constituent of the State.

It is often thought that Hegel means to give up the content of religious truth or to belittle it as unreal. Instead he meant to abide by it and establish it. To Hegel 'art, religion, and philosophy are Spirit's self-contemplative activity above and not below the self-objectifying will . . . They have one and the same rational content, which art expresses in the form of sense, religion in pictorial thinking, philosophy in explicitly rational form. This conception of a single content in three forms . . . clearly originates in his vision of ancient Athens, where for a dazzling half century patriotism, art and religion were fused in a happy totality of living, which to Hegel was above all the enjoyment of a divine beauty'.[1] Although 'the idea can find no demand of spirit unsatisfied in Christianity', the reformed religion itself must change its form from pictorial thinking to reason and become true philosophical knowledge of God as Spirit.[2]

Within his assumptions Hegel does full justice to religion. It is his assumptions that bring us to decision:

(i) Hegel undoubtedly overestimated 'imageless thought' as the form of reason that grasps Reality to the fullest extent open to men.

(ii) One of the far-reaching criticisms that emerged after Hegel's death was concerned with his insistence that he had propounded a philosophy of reconciliation in which all the criticisms were overcome. The critics emphasized that the

[1] *Op. cit.*, p. 184.   [2] *Op. cit.*, p. 200.

world as it existed contains many harsh contradictions that
are clearly unreconciled.

(iii) Hegel's assumption that art, religion and philosophy
have one and the same content inevitably distorts all
three.

(iv) As he sought to plumb the secrets of the developing
effects of the purpose of God in the universe, he was misled
by his anti-supernaturalism, not to acknowledge and find
greater depth and balance in recognizing the already existing
perfection of God.

(v) Though Hegel did more justice to the freedom and
responsibility of the individual than many suppose; but in
his attempt to do justice to the corporate life of men, the
individual is to some extent submerged.

(vi) In one sense Jesus Christ was central to Hegel's whole
philosophy as the symbol of that unity between God and
man, and that reconciliation between Infinite Spirit and
estranged nature, which it is the purpose of his philosophy
to portray. In another sense he was irrelevant, because
incarnation and reconciliation were in fact, according to
Hegel, writ large on the universe, not something wrought
out in an historic Incarnation whose effects have still to be
fully achieved.

With Hegel's death an epoch came to an end. It is often
contended that he built a system that cut off openness to the
future. But that was not his intention. He had built a
flexible system of perpetual movement. Certainly he thought
that he had established once for all *the method* by which
absolute spirit discloses itself in the finite. But the method
that Hegel had forged was used to attack him, and those who
followed him went in widely differing directions.

(c) *Attacks on Hegel's Synthesis*

(i) *Søren Kierkegaard* (1813–55). Kierkegaard protested
against Hegel's identification of thought and being, and in
opposition to it stressed the individual before God, the existing subject, who cannot be comprehended by the objective

intellect, and is to be distinguished sharply from the crowd, which is untruth.

Indeed, Kierkegaard went so far as to insist that faith, which is only gained by a leap, is the holding fast in the passion of inwardness but in objective uncertainty to what is absurd, and that this involves the crucifixion of the intellect.

So he says, 'A Christian clergyman who does not know how, with the passion of existential effort, to keep himself and the congregation in awe by proclaiming that the paradox cannot and shall not be understood, who does not affirm precisely that the task is to hold fast to this, and endure the crucifixion of the understanding, but has understood everything speculatively—that clergyman is comic.'[1] Faith involves not only the crucifixion of the intellect, but also 'the teleological suspension of the ethical'. This can be in the pattern of faith shown by Abraham's acceptance of the command of God to kill his son, though he knew it to be morally wrong.

Kierkegaard saw his problem as the task of clarifying the problem of becoming a Christian in a universal Christian civilization which was not, he thought, genuinely Christian. So he saw life as an 'Either-Or'. This is not masked by his conception of three *Stages on Life's Way*—the aesthetic (the objective, the uncommitted), the ethical, and the religious, because the ethical and the religious are essentially linked. The stages are distinguished existentially as enjoyment–perdition, action–victory and suffering. Transitions between them occur by leap—to the ethical by the need to act responsibly, to the religions through consciousness of sin. Kierkegaard drew a distinction between two kinds of religiousness—that whose characteristic is guilt, but whose inner dialectic does not lead to despair. The despair which is sin occurs only because of the contradiction that God has become man and because we can be offended at him.

For Kierkegaard truth is inwardness and subjectivity— known in passionate conviction, though it is absurd. Yet his

[1] *Unscientific Postscript*, O.U.P., 1941, p. 500.

subjectivity presupposed much that came from his interpretation of the Christian tradition. Christianity is something which must be held in obedient subservience to God's
majesty and not accommodated to popular opinion. God and
man are two qualities between which there is an infinite
qualitative difference. God is subject. The absurdity is that
God has come into being, has been born, has grown, and so on
precisely like any other human being. To Kierkegaard there
is no certainty in historical knowledge, and an essential contradiction between history and infinity. He says: 'To
require the greatest possible subjective passion, to the point
of hating father and mother, and then to put them together
with an historical knowledge which at its maximum can only
be an approximation—that is contradiction.'[1]

Over Kierkegaard's theology broods the melancholy of his
temperament. Suffering is for him the expression of the God-
relationship. He stresses anxiety, guilt and despair, bringing
acute psychological insight to the analysis of his own
experience. Guilt is the characteristic of all existence which is
marked by the leap from unconscious innocence.

Kierkegaard did a service in insisting on the gulf between
actual existence and any theoretical system. But his total
disjunction of the finite and infinite, objective and subjective,
reason and faith produced an inhuman result. Some synthesis of Kierkegaard and Hegel is desirable.

(ii) *Karl Marx* (1818–83). Karl Marx altered the background of Christian theology in three ways. First, while the
materialist theory of history is not the whole truth, it points
to the far-reaching influence of any economic background on
the thinking that is done within it. Secondly, Marx had a
conception of ideology—a word that is intrinsically neutral—
which made it the most dangerous weapon in the class
struggle.

He borrowed from Ludwig Feuerbach (1804–72) the conception that religion is a projection, caused by the individual
projecting his infinite desires outwardly, and related it to the

[1] *Op. cit.*, p. 510.

social situation which caused it. To Marx ideology was the unconscious production of ideas which justify the retention of power by those already in authority. This production happens unconsciously, but when those in authority become aware of the usefulness of the ideas, they can then also use them consciously to further their ends. Here again there is enough truth in this to put the theologian on his guard.

Thirdly, Marx propounded as his eschatological hope a perfect state of human society. This the Christian theologian should bear in mind, as he seeks to define the Christian conception of eschatology, that he may show to what extent it fulfils the Marxist hope.

(iii) *Friedrich Wilhelm Nietzsche* (1844–1900). Nietzsche's conception of ideology was different from that of Marx. He attributed the restraints on the emergence out of the mass of mankind of the new disciplined, vital, strong *Man*, to the resentment by the weak of the abilities and vital force of the strong. All universal standards, he thought, come from this source. Nietzsche is a perpetual reminder to the Christian theologian not to sentimentalize the Christian concept of 'love'.

Nietzsche's most famous utterance is: 'The greatest recent event—that "God is dead", that the belief in the Christian God has ceased to be believable—is even now beginning to cast its first shadows over Europe . . . We philosophers and "free spirits" feel as if a new dawn were shining on us when we receive the tidings that "the old god is dead"; our heart overflows with gratitude, amazement, anticipation, expectation.'[1]

In this Nietzsche did not think of himself as saying anything new. He accepted the teaching of Feuerbach as a final refutation of the claim of religion. He was only drawing a new inference. Since God is dead, the new man must emerge, the man full of unbroken vitality, in whom eternity is continuously present, to be the bearer of the new type of values

[1] From *The Gay Science*, Book V (1887): text given in *The Portable Nietzsche*, Walter Kaufmann (ed.), Viking Press, New York, 1954, pp. 447–8.

that human life needs. This again is an eschatology that should help the Christian theologian to define his own.

(d) *Theology Must Take Account of Biblical Criticism*

Ferdinand Christian Baur (1792–1860), in spite of the unsatisfactoriness of his conception of the relation between God and the universe, did two great services to Christian theology. In the first place, he insisted that the New Testament must be understood historically, and made his own stimulating controversial contribution to that understanding. For him, historical study had two different aspects, each of which had their own autonomy—an empirical (objective and critical) aspect, and a speculative (philosophical and theological) aspect. On the one side, no one has been more forthright than Baur in insisting that the Biblical scholar must not take anything for granted, but advance the knowledge of the truth without regard for consequences, and consider every book in the New Testament in relation to the historical circumstances of its origin. On the other side, he found it helpful to use the Hegelian dialectic to propound a theory that primitive Judaeo-Christianity was opposed by Paul and that the later writings of the New Testament show a reconciliation. For this theory he has been greatly criticized, but it was a great stimulus to research, and in the process of its refutation Biblical study made a great advance.

In the second place, he insisted that constructive Christian theology is intimately bound up with the understanding of the theology of the past. Here he set the pattern which has been followed. He wrote a historical study on the doctrine of the Atonement (1838), then one on the doctrine of the Trinity and the Incarnation (1841), then his textbook on the history of Christian Dogma (1847). His more important lectures on the history of Christian Dogma were published after his death in 1865–7. (Baur used the term 'history of dogma' in a very wide sense.) In these works we see the maturing of Baur's insight. The book on the Atonement gives a very unbalanced treatment, putting the whole

III] THE MAIN PROTESTANT DEBATE

development from primitive Christianity to the Reformation in one period, from the Reformation to Kant in a second, and making the post-Kantian period a complete section on its own. In Baur's final perspective, the first period covers the patristic age up to 604, divided at the Council of Nicaea; the second, the seventh to the fifteenth centuries with divisions at Gregory VII and at Anselm; the third from the Reformation to the present divided at the beginning of the eighteenth century. At a time when we need a more satisfying ecumenical perspective, our indebtedness to Baur needs to be recognized.

(e) *A Transitional Theological Construction*

Albrecht Ritschl (1822–89), in spite of his use of New Testament and wide-ranging historical studies, was essentially a constructive theologian. In revulsion from Idealism, a 'back to Kant' movement arose which was anti-metaphysical and moralistic. Ritschl endorsed this, and added to it an historical positivism. The combination met the mood of the time and dominated Protestant theology for nearly fifty years. His constructive theology is mainly set out in the third volume of his work—*The Christian Doctrine of Justification and Reconciliation* (1870–4)—*The Positive Development of the Doctrine: Justification and Reconciliation*.[1]

Ritschl staked everything on 'the correct and complete idea of the Christian religion' (p. 8; here the whole of § 2, pp. 8–14, is of determinative importance for the understanding and appraisal of Ritschl). He admitted that Schleiermacher was the first to adopt this method, but said that he did less than justice to the teleological character of Christianity and that he underestimated the religion of the Old Testament. Any criticism of Ritschl must come from denying the correctness of his definition of Christianity. It should be noted that much of his thinking is highly original and that his method is that of a discrimination between the essential and non-essential elements first in the New

[1] E.T., T. and T. Clark, 1902.

Testament and then in historical theology, and here not least in Luther, which enables him to use them in the service of the definition he is expounding.

This, then, is Ritschl's definition: 'Christianity . . . is the monotheistic, completely spiritual and ethical religion, which, based on the life of its Author as Redeemer and as Founder of the Kingdom of God, consists in the freedom of the children of God, involves the impulse to conduct from the motive of love, which aims at the moral organization of mankind, and grounds blessedness on the relation of sonship to God, as well as on the Kingdom of God' (p. 13).

Though this is not mentioned in the definition, Ritschl started from the basis of expounding the faith of the Christian community as a member of it. It is important to note this because Ritschl was implicitly presupposing the Christian faith as he theologized—not establishing the foundations, but altering traditional conceptions. In the definition there are four main concepts—God, Christ, the freedom of the children of God, and the Kingdom of God.

(i) *God.* It is plain from the definition that God exercises only an instrumental function in Ritschl's thinking. Fundamental to Ritschl's discussion of God is his conception of *value-judgments* (borrowed from Hermann Lotze (1817–81)). He said: 'Religious knowledge moves in independent value-judgments, which relate to man's attitude to the world, and call forth feelings of pleasure and pain in which man either enjoys the dominion over the world vouchsafed to him by God, or feels grievously the lack of God's help to that end' (p. 205). But in Ritschl's thinking this conception does not only apply to happenings in the world. It is the basis of his own thinking about God, in addition to what he takes for granted out of the faith of the Christian community. The result is that he made ontological judgments without accepting any responsibility for justifying them, and undertook no fundamental discussion on the nature and reality of God.

God for him is 'Loving Will' (p. 236), and 'a Person' (p.

228). His final end in the world is the Kingdom of God as the supreme good (p. 236), from which it is possible to explain the creation and government of the world. Justification of sinners must be 'referred to God under the attribute of Father' (p. 139). God 'is not conceived as being anything apart from and prior to his self-determination as love' (p. 282). And in this love there is no element of 'wrath' (p. 323) because 'sin is estimated by God, not as the final purpose of opposition to the known will of God, but as ignorance'. Once the immediate appeal of this, with its sense of deliverance from the oppressive bondage of traditional systems, passed, its unsatisfactoriness became apparent.

(ii) *Christ.* The phrase Ritschl used for Christ in his definition was 'the life of its author as Redeemer and as Founder of the Kingdom of God', and that expresses exactly Ritschl's achievement and its limitations. He rightly insisted that Christology must take seriously the life of Jesus as known by historical research, but he put Christology into a narrow historical strait-jacket. To Ritschl, Jesus was the historical founder of Christianity (p. 325), the prototype of man's vocation (p. 387) to share his relation to God and his attitude to the world (p. 386), and he brought the perfect revelation of God (p. 388). So he said: 'The twofold significance we are compelled to ascribe to Christ as being at once the perfect revealer of God and the manifest type of spiritual lordship over the world, find expression in the single predicate of his Godhead' (p. 389); and added: 'If Christ by what he has done and suffered for my salvation is my Lord, and if, by trusting for my salvation to the power of what he has done for me, I honour him as my God, then, that is a value-judgment of a direct kind' (p. 398).

Ritschl was here constricting Christology and its traditional terms within his own definition, which, he thought, gave all the religious reality possible. To criticism that he makes Christ only a mere man, he thought it sufficient to reply that by 'a mere man' he would mean man as a material entity apart from every characteristic of spiritual and moral personality, whereas it is clear that he has written of Christ in his personal character as the Bearer of the Revelation of God.

(iii) *The Freedom of the Children of God.* The phrase 'the freedom of the children of God' is a comprehensive description of what Ritschl meant by 'Justification and Reconciliation'. In this there is a double element 'freedom from guilt and over the world which is to be won through the realized Fatherhood of God' (p. 13).

Justification is the same as the forgiveness of sins, and it is 'the removal of guilt, and the consciousness of guilt, in so far as in the latter that contradiction to God which is realized in sin and expressed in guilt, works on as mistrust, and brings about moral separation from God' (p. 85). Ritschl took from Luther as the fundamental true attitude to God 'trust' (p. 333). He saw consciousness of guilt as expressing lack of fellowship with God, but this is for him dispelled when we simply realize that God is Father, and that he forgives sinners.

Freedom over the world is a distinctive and original conception of Ritschl's. Behind it lies a conception of 'the contradiction in which man finds himself, as both a part of the world of nature and a spiritual personality claiming to dominate nature' (p. 199). So he conceived reconciliation 'as the ground of deliverance from the world, and the ground of spiritual and moral lordship over the world' (p. 357). He saw Christ's patience under suffering as a test of his 'unique power over the world'. For the 'individual impulses of self-preservation, avoidance of pain, and the keeping inviolate of personal honour—impulses which in every case he subordinated to the consciousness of his vocation—imply, as their correlative term, the world as a whole'. Christians, following Christ, 'through faith in the loving providence of God, through the virtues of humility and patience, and finally through prayer' (p. 670), can achieve a similar lordship over the world. There is much truth in Ritschl's teaching on the point, but the nomenclature implies the unhappy antithesis between nature and spirit.

(iv) *The Kingdom of God.* It is absolutely essential to Ritschl's understanding of Christianity to join together reconciliation with God and moral action from the motive of love in fulfilment of our calling. The latter is an essential part of the Kingdom of God. He states the conjunction three times over in his definition (p. 13), and insists that they mutually condition each other (p. 668).

Ritschl's understanding of the Kingdom of God is essentially that of organized moral action. He said: 'In Christianity the Kingdom of God is represented as the common end of God and of the elect community in such a way that it rises above the natural limits of nationality and becomes the moral society of nations' (p. 10), and he insisted that Jesus meant by the Kingdom of God 'not the common exercise of worship but the organization of humanity through action inspired by love' (p. 12). Apart from his faulty understanding of the New Testament, Ritschl's thought suffers from his exclusion of the eschatological vision.

Ritschl deserves well of theologians for his pioneer attempt to take the historical life of Jesus seriously as a factor in Christian theology; but the foundations of his constructive effort are so faulty that he does not provide a basis for future construction.

(f) *The Place of Christianity Among the World Religions*

Ernst Troeltsch (1865–1923) may be included in the nineteenth century because he was the theologian of the 'historico-religious school' which stressed the interrelation between Christianity and other religions and which flourished from 1880 to 1920. He broke away from the narrow positivism of Ritschlianism, took a positive attitude to the developing science of comparative religion and thought that Christian theology should relate itself to it. But he remained essentially a Ritschlian in his central convictions and this prevented him from giving a satisfactory answer to the problems he raised. The basis of Troeltsch's thinking was his understanding of history. Here he formulated three laws which seemed to him to govern all historical inquiry:[1]

(i) *The law of criticism* in which he stressed that historical judgments are always open to revision and so, in his opinion, can only attain a greater or lesser degree of probability.

(ii) *The law of analogy* by which he meant that historical judgments presuppose an essential similarity between our humanity and the humanity of the past period.

(iii) *The law of inter-relatedness* by which he meant that to understand a historical event we must see it in terms of its antecedents and consequences and not separate it from its environment.

These are valuable general assumptions—but Troeltsch was too much under the bondage of the nineteenth-century understanding of scientific law. General assumptions must not dictate to the distinctive nature of actual events.

He himself used his understanding of history in exploring *The Social Teaching of the Christian Churches*.[2] Here he found two types of Christian civilization in which Christian ethical standards combined with social conditions to form a synthesis binding on all men, in contrast to what he thought the ascetic, world-denying view of the New Testament. These two types were the Medieval period, and the new unity of which '*Ascetic*' *Protestantism* was the core. From 1800 onwards Troeltsch thought that no such unity was possible because of the spread of religious individualism.

On the basis of his historical studies Troeltsch denied the 'absoluteness' of Christianity, because, in his judgment, it was not possible to say that Christianity had an 'essence'. This denial makes Christianity something that cannot be considered apart from particular social conditions.

His latest thinking is to be found in an essay *The Place of Christianity among the World Religions*.[3] He understood

[1] *Gesammelte Schriften*, Tübingen, J. C. B. Mohr, 1939, II, pp. 729–53.

[2] 1911, E.T., Allen and Unwin, 1931.

[3] E.T. in *Christian Thought: Its History and Application*, University of London Press, 1923.

Christianity as a personalistic religion which is the religion of Europeanism—what we would now call Western Civilization.

'Christianity,' says Troeltsch, 'could not be the religion of such a highly racial group if it did not possess a mighty spiritual power and truth, in short, if it were not, in some degree, a manifestation of the Divine Life itself. It is final and unconditional for us because we have nothing else, and because, in what we have, we can recognize the accents of the Divine Voice. But this does not preclude the possibility that other racial groups, living in their entirely different cultural conditions, may experience their contact with the Divine Life in a quite different way, and may themselves possess a religion which has grown up with them and from which they cannot sever themselves so long as they remain as they are' (p. 26).

Troeltsch's religious stance that lies behind this was essentially the instrumental one of Ritschl. 'The Christian position', Troeltsch affirmed, 'is maintained when we are conscious of the Father of Jesus Christ as a living presence in our daily conflicts, labours, hopes and sufferings, and when we arm ourselves in the power of the Christian spirit, for the weightiest decision in the world, the final victory of all eternal and personal values of the soul.'[1]

Troeltsch thus combined a massive sense of the inter-relation of all history, and the social conditioning of all religions, with a practical Christian faith which he had inherited. But he has provided no firm basis for the Christian faith he held, still less for his continuing to be Christian. Troeltsch is right in thinking that there is no simply objective demonstration of the place of Christianity among the world religions, but he has not grappled sufficiently with the problem of what Christians have a right and duty to affirm on their assumptions about the place of Christianity among world religions. This problem like others remains over from the nineteenth century for solution.

[1] *Zur Religiöse Lage: Religionsphilosophie und Ethik*, 1913, p. 440.

IV—THE TWENTIETH CENTURY

CHRISTIAN THEOLOGY IN SEARCH OF A NEW IDIOM OF CHRISTIAN FAITH

General Characteristics

'The nineteenth century', it was said, 'bequeathed its theological problems to its successor. If all human life is to be seen within a historical perspective, in what way is it now possible to affirm God transcendent incarnate in Christ? What is the nature of the Church, and under what conditions does it give trustworthy knowledge of God? What is the relation between Christianity and other religions? Can the truth of religion be a unifying factor in the life of mankind?' (p. 73).

These are still the unsolved theological problems of the twentieth century. But the twentieth century has given its own characteristic tang to their discussion. In it 'Christendom' as a presupposition has finally dissolved, and its inheritance survives only as powerful fragments. A secular civilization with immense technological power, which does not need the hypothesis of 'God' for its ordinary working, has emerged; and there is a clear breach between Christianity and the culture within which it seeks to live. In this context the overriding question is whether Christianity is in fact true, but this is clearly a live option.

In this situation there are four possible attitudes, and in the continuing debate they are all represented. It is possible to accept Christian truth as formulated by an earlier period and make minimal adjustments; or it is possible to respond to the contemporary situation in one of three ways: either (a) to be content with only such Christian thinking as harmonizes with contemporary cultural attitudes; or (b) to say that, with a little necessary adjustment, the full substance of authentic Christianity is compatible with the full rigour of contemporary cultural attitudes and the breach is non-existent; or (c) to seek to hold on to the Christian Gospel, and to work towards a way of thinking that is intellectually satisfying to Christian believers in the context of contemporary culture—and in so doing to be prepared, as Christian theologians in other centuries were, to see in Christian truth a source of intellectual illumination that causes thinkers to reject and modify as well as to accept contemporary assumptions.

But within this situation there are complicating factors. One is the Ecumenical Movement—that remarkable growing together of the different Christian communions which has fertilized theological study by promoting common discussion of central affirmations and exploration of historical differences and contemporary possibilities in a new way. But the ecumenical movement, for all its gains, is not the central fact of theological study in the twentieth century. However closely Christians come towards one another this fact of itself does not determine either the truth or the vitality of what they hold in common.

Where the Ecumenical Movement has been strong is in the probing of the nature of the Church and of its relation to society. A crucial decision was taken at the Lund Conference of Faith and Order 1952 'that the doctrine of the Church be treated in close relation both to the doctrine of the Christ and to the doctrine of the Holy Spirit' (*Report*, p. 11). This has been the direction of study ever since, and this study has been one of the factors behind the theology of the Second Vatican Council. It is evidenced in the *Report of the Uppsala Conference of the World Council of Churches* of 1968, especially in the report on 'The Holy Spirit and the Catholicity of the Church' which spoke of the purpose of Christ 'to bring people of all times, of all races, of all places, of all conditions into an

I

organic and living unity in Christ by the Holy Spirit under the Universal Fatherhood of God' (p. 13).

A notable statement on the Church's unity came out of the Delhi Conference of the World Council of Churches of 1961: 'We believe that the unity which is both God's will and his gift to his Church is being made visible as all in each place who are baptized into Jesus Christ and confess him as Lord and Saviour are brought by the Holy Spirit into one fully committed fellowship, holding the one apostolic faith, preaching the one Gospel, breaking the one bread, joining in common prayer, and having a corporate life reaching out in witness and service to all, and who at the same time are united with the whole Christian fellowship in all places and all ages in such wise that ministry and members are accepted by all, and that all can act and speak together as occasion requires for the tasks to which God calls his people' (*Report*, p. 116).

In addition the World Conference on Church and Society of 1966 expressed the conviction that Christian faith involves commitment to working for the transformation of the institutions of society (*Report*, p. 49). But the achievement of corporate unity has lagged behind the formulation of its theological necessity, and the Church is far from having found a confidently effective place in a rapidly changing technical society.

The impact of social conditions on the direction taken by theological study is in fact a major factor to be borne in mind in studying all twentieth-century theology. The influence of the two world wars of 1914–18 and 1939–45 was to draw attention to the darker aspects of man's nature, and to provoke the attempt at a new Christological theocentric affirmation of abiding Christian Truth. The influence of the threat of nuclear world destruction, combined with the increasingly rapid growth of technological achievement has erupted in the 1960s to produce a new atmosphere of uncertainty and conflicting tendencies. In a time of unceasing change can Christian theology reconsider its heritage and reassert Christian truth as true but in a new idiom? or will Christian theology destroy itself? or will the study of Christian theology fade away from lack of interest? Though the contemporary confusion is very great the Christian theologian can be in good heart.

1. *Orthodoxy*

Orthodox theology in the twentieth century represents a new expression of Orthodoxy open to the West in a new way —certainly to give, and up to a point to receive. In this it has been helped, not hindered, by the fact that the Revolution of 1917 forced a brilliant group of men to reaffirm the Orthodox tradition in a new setting.

The most notable figure of the older generation was Fr. Sergius Bulgakov (1871–1944) whose theological system was centred on Divine Wisdom (*sophia*). He used the term to express the resemblance of man to God. 'Man is created in the image of the divine *sophia*, and in this capacity he is himself determined as the creatively *sophia*: *sophia* in God is the principle of his self-revelation in the divine life . . . Moreover, this link between man and God in *sophia*, which forms the basis of human being, or of divine humanity, makes man at once capable of and called to accept divine revelation, makes him, in a word, the subject of revelation.'[1]

Bulgakov insisted that his thought was rooted in the thought of the Fathers, notably that of St. Basil the Great, St. John of Damascus and St. Maximus the Confessor. His theories were, however, found too speculative and theosophical by his younger contemporaries, Vladimir Lossky (1903–58) and Fr. George Florovsky (b. 1893), who have themselves shed vivid light on the historical process of the thinking of the Orthodox Church. All in all the controversy has helped to show the living relevance of patristic categories and traditions to the experience of the twentieth century.

[1] *Revelation*, J. Baillie and H. Martin (ed.), Faber and Faber, 1937, pp. 177–80.

A younger generation of thinkers has done great service in opening up the exploration of the history of Orthodox theology, and in expounding the characteristic Orthodox outlook (e.g. Alexander Schmemann (b. 1921), John Meyendorff (b. 1926), especially for his study of St. Gregory Palamas (*c.* 1296–1359), Nikos Nissiotis and Kallistos Timothy Ware (b. 1934)). In particular a new and important strand in the total field of theological discussion has come through the insistence on the greatness of the Byzantine period in theology; on the Christian humanism of the conception of *theosis*—the transformation and re-creation of mankind by the power of God; on the unity of the Church of all the centuries and of the present, in heaven and on earth, as a charismatic, individual and communal reality; and on the Liturgy as in outward richness and beauty an ikon of the Liturgy of Heaven and a foretaste of the unhindered rule of Christ.

For the full flowering of Orthodox theology we need a similar outburst of creative theological thinking from the Greek side of the Orthodox Church. Here are to be found some signs of new spiritual vitality, but not as yet the theology to which these may give rise.

Apart from making widely available theology texts in translation for study, the greatest need is for extensive Orthodox-Catholic theological discussion, because the rest of Christian thinkers would have a stake on both sides of the dialogue, and the result would be an enlargement of perspective in both East and West.

2. *Catholicism*

The great event affecting the theology of the Catholic Church has been the second Vatican Council of 1962–5. It occurred in what I have called (p. 157) 'the theological ferment of the sixties' and the resulting discussion is conditioned by that fact. It owed much to the genius of Pope John XXIII (1881–1963, Pope from 1958) who called it, and it sums up the fruits of the Biblical, patristic and liturgical

revival of the previous twenty or thirty years, which in turn
was in some measure fostered by Pope Pius XII (1876–1958,
Pope from 1939) as expressed in his encyclicals *Divino
Afflante Spiritu* (1943) on the study of the Bible, *Mystici
Corporis Christi* (also in 1943) on the Church and *Mediator
Dei* on the Liturgy. But the Council also initiated new
trends in theology due to the very fact of the meeting of the
Council and to the leadership first of Pope John and then
of Pope Paul VI. Assessment of the achievement of the
Council depends very largely on the future, on which elements
in the compromises worked out at Rome in 1962–5 become
dominant in succeeding years.

The Constitution on the Sacred Liturgy (promulgated 4th
December 1963) was the first document to be considered and
passed.[1] It set the direction of the Council in expressing the
central Christian convictions more biblically, stressing
corporate participation, emphasizing revision to bring out
more clearly the essential meaning and allowing some
adaptation to contemporary conditions and individual
cultures. The heart of the Liturgy was seen in the paschal
mystery which is the sacrament of Christ's death and resurrection celebrated by the Church, which is itself 'the sacrament of unity'.

Of great importance for assessing the achievement of the
Constitution on Liturgy are the permissive decisions:
communal celebration of rites is preferred, the use of the
mother-tongue and con-celebration may be extended, communion under both kinds may sometimes be allowed, and
some clerics may use a vernacular translation of the Divine
Office. Or the types of music besides Gregorian chant are
allowed, also the reverent use of contemporary art. Only
feasts of saints of universal importance are to be celebrated
by the Universal Church. Only the future can tell whether
the permissions will be widely acted upon, extended, or
withdrawn.

[1] A useful edition of the texts in translation is: *The Documents of Vatican
II*, Walter M. Abbott, S.J. (ed.), Geoffrey Chapman, 1966.

1964 saw the promulgation of the very important *Dogmatic Constitution on the Church* (21st November) and, on the same day, the *Decree on Ecumenism*, which showed a remarkable openness of the Catholic Church to fellowship and understanding with other Christians, and a recognition that in some sense they all belong within the one Church.

The first three chapters of the *Dogmatic Constitution on the Church* expound the three images which dominate the Council's thinking–the Church as 'Mystery', the Church as 'the People of God' and the Church as an institutional hierarchical structure. The first two chapters are Biblical rather than scholastic in texture:

Chapter I—*The Mystery of the Church*—asserts that 'by her relationship with Christ, the Church is a kind of sacrament or sign of intimate union with God'. 'This Church, constituted and organized in the world as a society, subsists in the Catholic Church, which is governed by the successor of Peter and by the bishops in union with that successor, although many elements of sanctification and of truth can be found outside her visible structure.' The Church 'like a pilgrim in a foreign land', presses forward amid the persecutions of the world and the consolations of God, announcing the cross and death of the Lord until He comes'.

Chapter II—*The People of God*—looks at the Church as a Messianic people. All its members, in their measure, participate in its essential life. All men are called to belong to it. And the Church recognizes that in many ways she is linked with those who are baptized, for many of them honour scripture, believe in God and Christ, and receive baptism and other sacraments within their own 'Churches or ecclesial communities'. In addition, those who have not received the Gospel are related to the People of God—Jews, Moslems, those who, though ignorant of the Gospel, sincerely seek God and even those who, though not aware of God, still strive to live a good life.

Chapter III—*The Hierarchical structure of the Church, with special reference to the Episcopate*—begins by reaffirming the teaching of Vatican I about the Pope, before expounding its teaching on bishops. Its theme here is that the authority of bishops is primarily sacramental rather than juridical. The chapter goes on to define the 'collegial authority' of bishops. The episcopal order is the subject of supreme and full power over the Universal Church, when united with its head, the Roman Pontiff, and acts with his consent. On the other hand, the Roman Pontiff, has free exercise of universal power over the Universal Church, solely in virtue of his office. It remains for the future to decide whether the collegiality of bishops can become fully real, so long as the Pope can exercise his power not only as head of the episcopal college but also apart from it, and above it. The Constitution includes a chapter on the role of the Blessed Virgin Mary, Mother of God, in the mystery of Christ and the Church. It turned away from thinking of Mary as a source of salvation, seeing her rather as the perfect exemplar of the Church to obedience. Many will welcome this emphasis, but there is still an unresolved division of conviction among Christians as to whether there is sufficient historical basis even for the typological conception of Mary.

The Decree on Ecumenism spelt out the implications of ecumenism for Catholics—first in 'ecumenical' action, the effort to eliminate unfair words, judgments and actions towards separated brethren, dialogue between different churches, closer co-operation for the common good, readiness for renewal and reform; and then in acknowledging the different degrees of relationship of the separated churches and ecclesial communities to the Roman Catholic Church. Here was openness towards other Christians of a new and remarkable kind.

Of the documents promulgated in the final session four are outstanding: *The Dogmatic Constitution on Divine Revelation* (1st November 1965); *The Pastoral Constitution on the Church in the Modern World* (7th December 1965); the *Declaration on the relationship of the Church to non-Christian religions*

(28th October 1965); and *The Declaration on Religious Freedom* (7th December 1965).

The Dogmatic Constitution on Divine Revelation begins, not with the distinction between scripture and tradition as was originally proposed, but with the one Revelation of the one God, but it is not a revolutionary document. It does, however, distinguish the truth of God from the literary forms in which it is expressed, and links together scripture, tradition, and the teaching authority of the Church.

The Pastoral Constitution on the Church in the Modern World was suggested by the Council itself and has corresponding merits and defects. It breathes a remarkable openness to the life of the world, with which the Church is to engage in mutually beneficial dialogue. But its detailed thinking shows no notable advance. It may be noted that the chapter on Marriage and the Family affirms that the parents must take the decisions about the begetting of children, but they must do so governed by a conscience dutifully conformed to the divine law interpreted by the Church. There is nothing here which precludes in any way the Papal encyclical *Humanae Vitae* of 1968 which prohibited the use of artificial contraceptives.

The little *Declaration on the relationship of the Church to non-Christian religions* breathed the same spirit of openness, this time to the non-Christian religions, even though it did not take the dialogue very far. It begins by insisting that the Church is giving deeper study to her relationship with non-Christian religions. These are graded according to their nearness to Christian truth—with Hinduism and Buddhism farthest away, Islam in the middle distance, and the Jews nearest in spiritual bond. The *Declaration* ends by repudiating as foreign to the mind of Christ any discrimination against men because of their race, colour, condition of life or religion. But the theological problem of religious differences in understanding the meaning of life remains unsolved.

The Declaration on Religious Freedom—On the right of the person and of communities to social and civil freedom in matters religious—is of outstanding importance as clinching the 'open' attitude of the Council. The substance of what is affirmed is given in the introduction, in which the Council admits that the concern for religious liberty has come to the Church from the world. It begins: 'A sense of the dignity of the human person has impressed itself more and more deeply on the consciousness of contemporary man. And the demand is increasingly made that men should act upon their own judgment, enjoying and making use of a responsible freedom, not driven by coercion, but motivated by a sense of duty. The demand is also made that constitutional limits should be set to the powers of government, in order that there may be no encroachment on the rightful freedom of the person and of associations. This demand for freedom in human society chiefly regards the quest for the values proper to the human spirit. It regards, in the first place, the free exercise of religion in society.'

The *Declaration* responds to this by saying: 'This Vatican Synod takes careful note of these desires in the minds of men. It proposes to declare them to be greatly in accord with truth and justice.' It added, somewhat unconvincingly, that this 'leaves untouched traditional Catholic doctrine on the moral duty of men and societies toward the one religion and toward the one Church of Christ'. But it also says quite clearly that 'the truth cannot impose itself except by virtue of its own truth, as it makes its entrance into the mind at once quietly and with power'.

The *Declaration* claims for all religious groups a comprehensive freedom including freedom of worship, of instruction, of gathering groups for fellowship, of training ministers, of communicating with religious authorities abroad, of erecting buildings and acquiring funds.

Four things are clear about the Vatican Council as a whole. First, the outstanding achievement of the Council was its manifestation of the openness of the Catholic Church to other Churches and ecclesial communities, to the world, and to the non-Christian religions. Secondly, the indispensable sign of this openness was the acknowledgment by the Council of freedom of conscience for individuals and for communities in religious matters as something rooted in the essential dignity of human life, and supported by the teaching of the Christian religion, if not always by its practice. Thirdly, the Council exhibited a remarkable attempt to subordinate the juridical element in the life of the Church to the sacramental quality of the pilgrim people of God. The crucial question that this raises for any Christian doctrine of the Church is: What is the right understanding of the teaching authority of the Church? Fourthly, the permission for alterations in Church practice showed ways in which the openness asserted by the Council can be translated into actual fact, if the permitted alterations are acted upon or even extended.

The work of individual theologians may be illustrated by four names:

(a) In the early years of the century Baron Friedrich von Hügel (1852–1925) exercised as a layman a wide influence, though mainly among non-Catholics. He was born in Florence, where his father was Austrian ambassador, but came to England in 1867, where he spent most of his life. He was closely associated for many years with the Catholic Modernists who were condemned in 1907 and fully shared their sense that theology should take full account of the historical process and make use of scientific methods of historical criticism. (He stressed the need to hold together the contributions of Greece, with its unceasing intellectual quest and its use of logic; of Christianity, with its sense of spiritual mystery and value of personality, and its answer in Christ to man's God-given search for God; and of natural science, with its discipline of observations of facts and the detection of their interrelation.)

But he turned away from Catholic Modernism at the point where it seemed to him to deny the divine transcendence. As over against any exclusive stress on the divine immanence he insisted that God is to be 'apprehended, loved, and served by us neither as Process nor as Product, but as overflowing Being, as Perfect Reality, as the Real Ideal'. 'In His Will— His nature and Being as they already are, as they ever have been, not in any Becoming of Him, but in the Being of Him' —'in His Will is our peace'.[1]

(b) In the 1950s the works of Marie-Joseph-Pierre Teilhard de Chardin, S.J. (1881–1955), began to be published. He was a distinguished geological and palaeontological scholar who did much of his research in China. The authorities of his order prevented publication of his work until after his death, because of the speculative character of his attempt to unite evolutionary science and Christian theology.

He was first and foremost a priest, and his most striking testament is a book of devotion *Le Milieu Divin*.[2] He expressed the heart of his spirituality in a syllogism: 'at the heart of our universe, each soul exists for God, in our Lord. But all reality, even material reality, around each one of us, exists for our souls. Hence, all sensible reality around each one of us, exists, through our souls, for God in our Lord' (p. 56). This principle he affirmed because he believed that through the suffering Incarnation of Christ God enables us to harness for him the spiritual power of matter (p. 107). We need to link together the thread of our inward development which moulds our ideas, affections and attitudes, and the thread of outward events by which the whole sum of the forces of the universe meet together to work in us the effect which God desires (p. 79). Indeed, he says 'to desire the Parousia, all we have to do is to let the very heart of the earth, as we Christianise it, beat within us' (p. 154). In affirming this, he is not unaware of evil, sin and death. He thinks that not only our unavoidable ills but even our most deliberate faults, and death itself, which forms an essential part of our lives, can be embraced in God's transfiguration by

---

[1] *Essays and Addresses in the Philosophy of Religion*, Second Series, Dent, 1926, p. 202.
[2] E.T., first published in 1957, Fontana, 1964.

which he incorporates them in a better plan—'provided we
lovingly trust in him' (p. 86).

He united his personal devotion and his scientific work in a
Christ-centred evolutionary vision of the universe as a whole.
The universe will ultimately converge on the 'omega-point'
—a supra-personal unity of all things in God. Christ is
the expression of that omega-point within the continuing
process. The cosmological law of the evolutionary process is
that with increasing complexity of physical organization
goes an increase in the purposefulness of life and consciousness. Man is now responsible for the direction of evolution
which continues at the spiritual and social level. Mankind
will eventually become fully united and personal through
love—the highest expression of radial energy. In this process
God, made known in Christ, will draw all things towards
perfection in himself.

Christian theology must express this Christ-centred vision
of the universe. It must see God in his transcendent personal
being in hierarchical union with the universe, and work out
the evolution of the whole Christ (the Church as the mystical
body of Christ) in the process of human evolution.

Teilhard's vision certainly has exercised a wide appeal. Its
integration into the corpus of philosophical and theological
thinking is another matter. It has been noted that on this
basis sin tends to be limited to a shortcoming in the evolutionary process, and that eschatology remains vague. But
Teilhard's thinking is an urgent plea for the theologian to see
that his theology really affirms Christ as the Lord of the
universe.

(c) One of the most massive of philosophical theologians is
another Jesuit, Karl Rahner (b. 1904), who combines un-
swerving obedience to the Catholic Church with an inde-
fatigable endeavour to think through the existential meaning
of Catholic scholastic theology at the present day. His
approach is anthropological, but he finds the essence of man
in his transcendence as spirit, which relates him to holy
mystery, even when he is not conscious of it. Holy mystery

belongs to God solely and primarily as the Whither of
transcendence. The freedom of man's mastery of things
comes from his being mastered by the holy which is itself
unmastered.[1]

Rahner's essential fidelity to Catholicism can be seen in his
treatment of the development of dogma (Vol. I, pp. 39–77),
for example, in the doctrine of the bodily assumption of the
Virgin Mary, which has not always been in existence as an
explicit statement. Rahner believes that authentic identity
and really genuine development can be reconciled. This is
because the Church possesses in the magisterium an organ of
perception by which she can tell whether something, which
from our point of view emerges as a result of theological
speculation is, objectively, God's word in a new articulation
(Vol. I, p. 75).

On the other hand, he makes several exploratory suggestions which point to his influence on Vatican II. For
example, he thinks of mankind as a unity, and of the existence
of a 'people of God' extending as far as all humanity and
before its social and juridical organization in a Church (Vol.
II, p. 83). Further, he stresses the function of the Pope as
head of the episcopal college, and argues that even where the
Pope acts in his own person he acts as the head of the episcopate as a whole (Vol. V, p. 249). Thirdly, he has a generous
attitude towards non-Christian religions and believes that
God can be victorious by his secret grace even where the
Church does not win the victory but is contradicted (Vol. V,
p. 134).

A different type of thinker is Hans Küng (b. 1928), who
has striven for *rapprochement* with other Christians and,
apart from a massive sympathetic confrontation of the
teaching of Karl Barth on Justification with Catholic teaching, has gathered up his studies in his book *The Church*.[2] In
this, while remaining firmly in the Roman obedience, he

---

[1] *Theological Investigations*, E.T., Darton, Longman and Todd, Vol. IV,
1966, pp. 52–4.
[2] 1967, E.T., Burns and Oates, 1967.

went to the limit in subordinating the institutional to the charismatic. Küng found the fundamental structure of the Church in its existence as the People of God, the Creation of the Spirit, and the Body of Christ. He interprets the attributes of one, catholic, holy and apostolic in his own way. He thinks that the New Testament demonstrates that the unity of the Church is a unity in plurality and diversity (p. 96), that to be truly catholic the Church must think of itself not as synonymous with the world, nor yet on the other hand as an exclusive society of those already saved, but as an open community of people dedicated to serve and work for the salvation of mankind (p. 319), that the Church is sinful as well as holy, but the foundation of its faith, the root of its love, the basis of its hope will remain untouched, and that apostolicity, i.e. becoming true successor of the apostles, must continually be achieved afresh (p. 358).

In addition, the ministry of ecclesiastical office is rooted in the priesthood of all believers—the priestliness of the whole people of God (p. 372). Küng sees the crown of the ecclesiastical structure in the Papacy, but he admits that 'from the Middle Ages onwards, and throughout modern times the official Catholic ecclesiology was an ecclesiology of apologetics and reaction' (p. 448). He pins his hopes on the epoch-making turning-point of the Papacy of John XXIII, in which the Primacy was seen as a 'call to serve his brethren inside and outside the Catholic Church, which must be inspired by love and understanding for mankind in the modern world and subject to the true Lord of the Church (p. 450). Küng's theology of the Church, if accepted within his own Church, opens up the possibility of wide agreement.

3. *Christianity in Britain*

British Christianity up to the 1960s may be focused in five representative figures: John Oman (1860–1939), Peter Taylor Forsyth (1848–1921), William Temple (1881–1944), John Baillie (1886–1960) and Donald Macpherson Baillie (1887–1954).

John Oman represents at its best the liberal theology that was dominant in the early years of the century. His constant insistence all through his work is that 'in religion we must be as bold, as free, as honest to face all realities as in science and religion'.[1] He set his problem in his early work *The Problem of Faith and Freedom in the Last two Centuries* in this way: 'The ultimate problem of at least the last two centuries I take to be the relation of faith and freedom, the problem of how faith is to be absolute and freedom absolute, yet both one'.[2] For him the essential quality of a religious person is to be absolutely dependent and that of a moral person is to be absolutely independent. Both, he held, are essential in our response to God the Father, who always deals with us in a personal way. Jesus Christ is 'the one unblurred mirror' (p. 194) of God's gracious relation to his children; and, if we say that we believe in him, we must stand for what he stood for.[3]

The culmination of his thinking was his book on *The Natural and the Supernatural*, a massive survey of the whole field of religion which he saw as culminating in the prophetic type.[4] He himself drew attention to the last paragraph as summing up his teaching: 'If we would have any content in the eternal, it is from dealing whole-heartedly with the evanescent; if we would have any content in freedom it is by victory both without and within over the necessary; if we would have any content in mind and spirit we must know aright by valuing aright. If so, religion must be a large experience in which we grow in knowledge as we grow in humility and courage, in which we deal with life and not abstractions, and with God as the environment in which we live and move and have our being, and not as an ecclesiastical formula. This we realize, as environment is only to be realized, by rightly living in it' (p. 471).

---

[1] *Honest Religion*, Cambridge University Press, 1941, p. 51.
[2] Hodder and Stoughton, 1906, p. 4.
[3] *Grace and Personality*, Cambridge University Press, 1917, rev. edn., 1925.
[4] Cambridge University Press, 1931.

The weakness of John Oman's theology lies in his over-tight unity between faith and freedom. This meant that he assumed the content of faith which he took to be valid, without justifying it. He took for granted the Christian tradition in its prophetic aspect, the Fatherhood of God, and Jesus as the complete response to him. While he presupposed the existence and necessity of the Church, he had no patience with its institutional life, and his appeal was constantly to the insight and integrity of the individual. Though stressed the personal character of God, he shared with Schleiermacher, whose *Speeches* he translated in 1893, a tendency to make no clear distinction between God and the order of reality. His theory of the holy as reverence by which we are set free to deal with the natural environment suffers from misrepresenting the teaching of Rudolf Otto (1869–1937) on the Holy. In fact, Otto gave as much place to the rational and moral element in the numinous as Oman did.

By contrast with John Oman, his older contemporary, P. T. Forsyth was remarkable for combining a full acceptance of the liberal tools of research and criticism, with a repudiation of what seemed to him a sentimentalizing of the meaning of the Fatherhood of God and of the sin of man in the theology which had been built upon the results of their use.

His basic question was that of the preacher: 'How is the revelation "God is love" made effective by God?' His answer was that Christ's death altered from God's side the whole relation between God and man for ever. God's love is love in holy action, and his holiness makes sin damnable as sin and love active as grace. Christ confessed the holiness of God. He could not confess the guilt of sin in the same sense, but in sympathetic identification with man's self-condemnation, he felt the wrath of the Holiest against sin. In this he made expiatory atonement for mankind, and gave moral penetration to the preaching of the Gospel.[1]

---

[1] *Positive Preaching and Modern Mind*, Hodder and Stoughton, 1909, Chapter IX.

In the act of atonement is expressed the moral power of the Incarnation rooted in the decision of God to act as Redeemer, to be born, suffer and die. In doing so, God limits himself in the power of holiness for the purposes of his own end of infinite love. Nothing impairs the reality of the human life of Christ, the conditions of its finitude, the necessity of growth within time. The sinless growth of Christ's character is the gradual act of God. This we can affirm, but *how* the Eternal God could make the condition of human nature his own we do not know.[1] Forsyth's theology, though not immediately effective, was later valued highly, but its intellectual construction, built on moral passion, though stimulating, and a warning against shallow theologies, does not grapple with the intellectual problems which had emerged by the 1960s.

William Temple's greatest work is his Gifford Lectures, *Nature, Man and God*.[2] His concern was to construct a Christian metaphysic showing the universe as an ascending series of levels—matter, life, mind and spirit—with the Incarnation as the climax of the series. In this he saw evil not as merely an apparent blemish, but as a real discord only justified when it had in fact produced greater good. Towards the end of his life, under the imminence of the war of 1939–45, he admitted that a greater emphasis on eschatology was necessary, but he still hoped that in a serener time Christian theology would return to its task of constructing a Christian metaphysic.

On the Incarnation itself, he repudiated a kenotic Christology but did not remove the need for it. He emphasized the cost of the Cross to God. On the Church he said that contemporary Christendom was not the source of authority to minister in the name of the Universal Church. This was handed down by the episcopal order. But he acknowledged other real ministries within the Universal Church.

---

[1] *The Person and Place of Jesus Christ*, 1st edn., 1909, Independent Press, 1930, Chapters X–XII.
[2] Macmillan, 1934.

K

Through his teaching that Revelation comes in the
coincidence of event and its true interpretation he helped
theologians to discard the theory of a body of revealed
propositions standing in its own right. A more complex
theory doing justice to all the factors involved and not
neglecting the propositional element is still needed. Characteristic of his mind is his insistence that 'the essential
principle of spiritual authority is the evocation by Good of
appreciation of itself'; and that 'the spiritual authority of
God Himself consists not in His having the power to create
and to destroy, but in His being the appropriate object of
worship and love'.[1]

John Baillie's theology changed in mid-course from an
emphasis on Religion to one on Revelation. His early major
work was *The Interpretation of Religion*.[2] It was written in
1922–5 and published in 1929. In it he attempted to construct a science of religion that should elucidate the meaning
of the religion of the whole human race, making a special
study of German Protestant theology from Hegel to Herrmann. He defined religion as a moral trust in reality, and
found belief in God necessary to its maintenance. The
criterion of truth and falsity in religion lay in the satisfaction
offered to our moral consciousness. Religion reaches its
climax in the Cross of Christ. The work ends with a consideration of the idea of Revelation. To our human activity
of faith, there has always seemed to correspond a divine
activity of grace. The long history of divination culminates
in the doctrine of the divinity of Jesus Christ. But Revelation
and Incarnation are no unique historical prodigies but are
by God's grace, of the very warp and woof of our human
experience.

In a later work *And the Life Everlasting*,[3] he found only
four possibilities before human life—two dead: tribalism with
its purely corporate ethic and immortality, and Brahminism
with its reabsorption of all finite spirits into one general fund

[1] *Op. cit.*, pp. 345, 349. [2] T. and T. Clark.
[3] O.U.P., 1934.

of spiritual life; but two living: either a radical pessimism or the hope of everlasting life with God.

In 1939 under the stimulus of Barth and Brunner he wrote a new book on God's self-disclosure—*Our Knowledge of God*.[1] He had come to think that there was need for a new emphasis on the transcendence of God; but he insisted that this should be done without denying some truth in the thought of divine immanence. His basic affirmation was that all religion testifies to the confrontation of the human soul with the transcendent holiness of God. This means that all men know God directly (even if they are not aware of it). This direct knowledge is a mediated immediacy—mediated by the presence of other people and the created world, and especially by history with its centre in Jesus Christ. Intellectual denial of God's existence is less serious than the practical denial of his claims, but an unabridged Christian profession and practice is necessary for the fullness of spiritual life.

His posthumously published Gifford Lectures *The Sense of the Presence of God*[2] illustrate but do not advance the argument. John Baillie's Christian stance prevented him doing justice to the whole field of religion; nor does his doctrine of Christian Revelation express its full complexity. The stress on perception in the awareness of God needs to be balanced by one on venture.

His brother, Donald Baillie, was more of a dogmatic theologian. His early book *Faith in God and its Christian Consummation*[3] rooted faith in a wide sense in moral experience and linked together theology and psychology. He used the concept of paradox to grasp the contrast between the terrible reality of evil and the Father of infinite power, wisdom and love revealed in the Gospel of Jesus Christ.

This concept of paradox he developed in his most famous work *God was in Christ*[4]—a beautifully written work. He stressed the need for real knowledge of the Jesus of history,

---

[1] Oxford University Press.   [2] O.U.P., 1962.
[3] T. and T. Clark, 1927; Faber and Faber, 1964.
[4] Faber and Faber, 1948; 2nd edn., 1955.

and for thinking through the meaning of the Christian conviction that God was incarnate in Jesus. He appealed to the paradox of grace, and affirmed that the same type of paradox, taken at the absolute degree, makes the life of Jesus the life of a man and yet also the very life of God incarnate (p. 129). In the last resort this approach evades the intellectual difficulty of the Incarnation, because it dismisses as an artificial distinction, Thomas Aquinas' distinction between habitual grace, given to Christ as man, like other men, and the grace of union, given only to Christ (p. 138).

Donald Baillie's posthumously published lectures on *The Theology of the Sacraments*[1] constituted an eirenical thinking out of the justification of sacraments to bridge the gulf between Protestant and Catholic positions. True spirituality which affirms the reality of personal life is helped not hindered by the use of material signs; and it is better to say that sacraments *operate through* human faith, rather than that they depend on it.

4. *Christianity in America*

American Christianity up to the sixties, leaving out the influence of Paul Tillich who will be treated in the next section, may be represented by four names: William Newton Clarke (1841–1912); Walter Rauschenbusch (1861–1918); Reinhold Niebuhr (b. 1892) and Helmut Richard Niebuhr (1894–1962).

Clarke's *Outline of Christian Theology*[2] is a superbly clear and confident expression of Liberal Theology. He acknowledged two sources of theology: Christian revelation (the self-expression of God) and the universe. In the Old Testament there is a gradual discovery of God. Christ is the unique expression of God's character and will. Christianity is in agreement with the primal certainties of the human spirit; its superiority to other religions lies in the effectiveness of its

[1] Faber and Faber, 1957.

[2] First published in 1898. Twenty editions had been published by 1914; T. and T. Clark, 1899.

moral transformation of human life. The discovery of God comes through the religious nature of man, through the dilemma of a good or a bad God, and through the spiritual experience of men especially in Christianity. Sin is that for which man was not created and to which he is not adapted. The Incarnation is possible because of the kinship between man and God. In Christ's reconciling work, love suffers in saving, and God bears in order that he may save. The Resurrection is vital but not the manner of it. In the section on the Holy Spirit and the divine life in man there are only five pages on the Church. The section on *Things to Come* affirms a blessed state beyond this life, the possibility of moral change within it, and the hope that God will save all men.

Walter Rauschenbusch is notable not as a theologian but for injecting into Liberal Theology awareness of the appalling problems of industrial society. In his book *A Theology for the Social Gospel*[1] he found the key to the Gospel in the goal of the Kingdom of God defined as humanity organized according to the will of God. This included mission, pastoral care, teaching, church union, political achievement and the reorganization of the industrial system. He insisted that theology by neglecting the kingdom of God has kept Christian people from fully realizing how social sins frustrate its coming. He laid stress on 'the kingdom of evil'—the corporate aspect of human wickedness—but did not relate it to individual sin and salvation. The union between the Gospel and social concern remained a personal one but not a theological one. His thought was evolutionary and optimistic and in the midst of war he died disappointed. But he focused in his vivid utterance a social concern that Christian theology could not afterwards ignore.

Reinhold Niebuhr, who reflected the changed attitude of the middle years of the century and contributed to it, is difficult to assess because his thought continually developed. He often insisted that he was no theologian, and this is

[1] Macmillan, New York, 1917.

reflected in the lack of precision in his concepts. But he did provide more of a theology for the social Gospel.

Basically he attempted to show that the Biblical understanding of man, taken seriously but not literally, is truer to the historical experience of human life than either Marxism or liberalism. No purely rational account of man, but only one with a framework of meaning and mystery can do justice to the realities of human life where it transcends itself, such as the freedom and responsibility of the self, its sin and guilt, and the unity of its freedom and its physical organism (see *The Self and the Dramas of History*).[1]

Niebuhr's early experience as a minister in Detroit in 1915–28 undermined his initial optimism and gave him an insight into the harshness and pretences of the industrial system. So he came to insist that in every human group there is less capacity for transcendence, and therefore more unrestrained egoism than in the individuals which compose it.[2]

In his Gifford Lectures on *The Nature and Destiny of Man*,[3] having come to learn from Augustine, Niebuhr developed a theory of sin and original sin. He saw sin as pride and that it arose out of the inevitable tendency in man to transcend his insecurity and his ignorance. But although it is inevitable it is not necessary, and man acknowledges his responsibility by his sense of guilt.

The question was, he thought, whether there are resources in the heart of the Divine Nature which can overcome the tragic character of history and which can cure as well as punish the sinful pride in which man inevitably involves himself. These he found in the sacrificial love of God revealed in the Cross of Christ and in the certainty of resurrection— the divine consummation of history which man, of himself, cannot achieve. These enable Christians to live a life of love, sensitive to their own need for transformation and con-

[1] Faber and Faber, 1956.
[2] *Moral Man and Immoral Society*, Scribner, 1932.
[3] Nisbet, 1941, 1943.

stantly working to make the structures of society more able
to nourish truly human living.

Niebuhr's theory of the sinfulness of corporate institutions
and of the need to work constantly for structural trans-
formations while pinning our hopes too much to them, has
been widely accepted. This is not true of his theory that sin
is inevitable but not necessary. He was right in insisting
against Karl Barth that affirmation of Christian truth needs
to be combined with a wide understanding of experience, but
he left the foundations of Christian faith needing more
searching investigation.

His younger brother, Helmut Richard Niebuhr, insisted
that his work revealed the combined influence of Karl Barth
and Ernst Troeltsch. He took the understanding of revelation
from the one and the emphasis on the relativity of history on
the other. In his most famous work *Christ and Culture*[1] he
expanded Troeltsch's three types of Christian civilization—
the church type, the sect type and individual mysticism—
into five: with the extremes 'Christ against Culture' and 'the
Christ of Culture', and three mediating types. Of these latter:
one is synthetic, though it acknowledges a higher order than
culture in Christ; one is dualistic, stressing the dualism even
while holding the two elements together; and the third is
conversionist, stressing the power of Christ to transform
culture and make it serve his purposes. Niebuhr had most
sympathy with the conversionist type, but he recognized that
there is no one Christian answer, and that the actual situation
determines the kind of response to the kind of attitude
which under differing circumstances the Christian ought to
adopt.

Richard Niebuhr's probing of the question of revelation
occurred mainly in two works—*The Meaning of Revelation*[2]
and *Radical Monotheism and Western Culture*.[3] In these he
never broke free from the limitations of his mentors—either
from the revelational positivism of the one or the cultural

[1] Faber and Faber, 1952.   [2] Macmillan, New York, 1941.
[3] Faber and Faber, 1961.

relativity of the other. In the earlier one he affirmed that Christian theology can only begin from faith in God's Revelation known in Christian history in which God discloses himself to us as our knower, our author, our judge and our only saviour (p. 182). In the latter he saw a conflict in Western culture between Radical Monotheism—between the knowledge of the principle of being as the valuing and saving power in the world (p. 43), and social faith which makes a finite cultural or religious society the object of trust as well as of loyalty (p. 11). But he refused to justify his essential position, and he bequeathed the problem to later discussion.

5. *The Main Protestant Debate*

The main Protestant debate has taken place in the German-speaking area, and four names are outstanding: Adolf von Harnack (1857–1930), Karl Barth (1886–1968), Rudolf Bultmann (b. 1884) and Paul Tillich (1886–1965).

Adolf von Harnack represents the Liberal Theology that was dominant in the early years of the century. He was an historical scholar of immense erudition. He believed that the purpose of studying history is in order to be able to intervene effectively in contemporary history. In two ways he focused his theological outlook—first through his massive *History of Dogma*[1] and second through his popular lectures *What is Christianity?*[2]

Harnack understood by dogma those ecclesiastical doctrines concerning the person and work of Christ which every Christian had to accept if he was to be in communion with the Church. He sought to show how the Gospel, which, in his understanding, had nothing to do with ecclesiasticism and authoritative doctrine, became institutionalized. He believed that the Patristic Christology represented the Hellenization of the Gospel, necessary to commend it to that age, but burdensome to later ages. The Reformation was essen-

[1] Three vols., 1886–9; E.T., 7 vols., 1894–9; 7 vols. in 4, Dover Press, 1961.
[2] 1898, E.T., 1899; Harper Torchbook, 1957.

tially a rediscovery of the Gospel, and an assertion of its
centrality. Unfortunately, as he thought, this was combined
with the preservation of the Patristic dogma. To be faithful
to the Reformation meant to continue reforming and to free
Christianity from doctrinal authoritarianism.

In his popular lectures he gave to many the impression
that he thought that the Gospel is simply the teaching of
Jesus freed from its eschatological setting, but this does not
do justice to him. It is fairer to say that it consists of two
elements and that it has one of its early fruits constantly
associated with it. The two elements are: 1—'the glad
message of the government of the world and of every
individual soul by the almighty and holy God, the Father and
Judge'.[1] 2—Jesus Christ is the 'personal realization and
strength of the Gospel'. The early and permanent fruit of
the Gospel is 'the Easter faith'—'the conviction that the
crucified one gained a victory over death'. 'Belief in the
living Lord and in a life eternal', said Harnack, 'is the act of
the freedom which is born of God.'[2]

Fundamental to Harnack's procedure is the selection of
the distinctive essence from the temporary historical forms
in which it is clothed—and this applies to the New Testament
as much as to later theology. In doing this he by-passed the
eschatological character of the New Testament. The practical
meaning of Christianity was simply 'eternal life in the midst
of time, by the strength and under the power of God'.[3]
Towards the end of his life he campaigned for three things—
the repudiation of the Old Testament as a canonical authority,
a new confessional affirmation of the lordship of Christ which
left speculation free, and an undogmatic Christian unity. In
his preface to the English edition of his *History of Dogma*
Harnack wrote: 'In taking up a theological book we are in the
habit of enquiring first of all as to the "standpoint" of the
author. In a historical work there is no room for such
enquiry.' But he was mistaken. His historical work is

---

[1] *History of Dogma*, I, p. 58. [2] *Op. cit.*, pp. 160–3.
[3] *What is Christianity?*, p. 8.

directed by an unexamined theological stance which needs justification.

Against the Liberal Theology represented by Harnack came a violent reaction initiated by Karl Barth. The war of 1914–18 was a profound shock to him. He was horrified to find his Liberal Protestant teachers endorsing the ethical standpoint of the German emperor, and this led him to question their whole theology and to look in the Bible for an authentic word of God as he sought to preach to his Swiss congregation under the shadow of war. He read Kierkegaard who led him to Luther and Calvin and Dostoievsky. He discovered what he called 'the strange new world of the Bible', and found out that you do not speak of God by speaking of man in a loud voice. He came to believe that there was no road from man to God, and that man's religion, as much as any other aspect of human life, left him self-enclosed. But into man's world God spoke and came, coming not horizontally but vertically, striking paradoxically and shatteringly into the world of man's pride and presumption.

The outcome of this period was Barth's *Commentary on the Epistle to the Romans*,[1] in which the paradoxical character of his new awareness of God in which 'redemption is invisible, inaccessible, impossible, for it meets us only in hope' found passionate and striking expression. The impact of this book—whether it horrified, or was welcomed, or seemed a one-sided version of an attitude that needed to be recovered—changed the emphasis in theological reflection and discussion from an anthropocentric one to a theocentric one.

This extreme eschatological position of Barth lasted only till about 1925. Then his thinking and achievement changed to the construction of a vast, and flexible, and unfinished *Church Dogmatics* (1932–67),[2] centred in Christology, with many original features in which there is a considerable amount of what he called 'theological exegesis', and a running

[1] 1918, E.T., 6th edn., O.U.P., 1933.
[2] E.T., T. and T. Clark, 1956–69.

dialogue with the past history of theology and with contemporary discussion, in the service of theological construction. In this the links between God and man—though established only from God's side—are real.

A fine expression of the starting-point of Barth's *Church Dogmatics* is to be found in the first article of *The Theological Declaration of the Synod of Barmen* of 31st May 1934, for which he was largely responsible. This read: 'Jesus Christ, as he is attested to us in Holy Scripture, is the one Word of God, which we have to hear, and which we have to trust and obey in life and death.'

For Barth, the starting-point of all theological construction was the concrete fact of the incarnate Christ, and he worked out as never before in history what it means to have a theology in which everything—everything whatever—is derived from the grace of God in Christ. Here we learn that God is for man, and that in all that God does for man God remains sovereignly free, and that his action is always the action of his grace. On this basis, the structure of the theology he erected is essentially simple, despite its voluminousness—The Word of God, God, God the Creator, God the Reconciler, God the Redeemer.

Three aspects of Barth's theology are specially determinative:

(a) Of crucial importance was his attitude to Revelation and the Bible. Revelation he limited to the Revelation of God in Jesus Christ. This meant two things—first, that he repudiated completely 'natural theology', and that he repudiated also all religion except that based on faith in Jesus Christ. Behind Barth's theology lay an extremely sceptical view of human thinking and activity. True relation between God and man can come about only from God's side. One of the aspects of human thinking about which Barth is extremely sceptical is the religious, and in the second half-volume of the first volume of his *Church Dogmatics* he devoted one large section to '*The Revelation of God as the Abolition of*

Religion'. The Church is the locus of true religion, but only so far as through grace it lives by grace.

Not only is Revelation limited to the Revelation known in Christ but this Revelation is made known through the Bible without human distortion. Here the divine communicates itself without the human element interfering. Historical criticism Barth knew through and through in his incessant dialogue with contemporary thinking, but in the end he let the text as it is speak to him without probing behind the text to its historical foundation or judging its truth. His theology is not based on history but on the Word of God. Barth's description of his own method of writing theology is this: 'At each point I listen as unreservedly as possible to the witness of Scripture and as impartially as possible to that of the Church, and then consider and formulate what may be the result.'[1] But this would-be consistent attempt to repudiate the human element and concentrate on divine grace which alone is trustworthy, cannot take away the fact of human assessment or ensure that the result is uncontaminatedly God's truth. Yet there is no doubt that this teaching had beneficial effects on Biblical study leading thinkers to probe the theological content of the Bible, in addition to the work of literary and historical criticism.

(*b*) Barth took his stand on the concrete fact of God's Revelation in Jesus Christ, and from this point developed God's dealing with his whole creation in creation, reconciliation and redemption. But he insisted straight away that this revelation required a Chalcedonian Christology and an Augustinian-style doctrine of the Trinity. As he saw it, according to the witness of the Bible, Jesus Christ reveals himself to be the incarnate Word of God, and so very God and very man, and also as Son of the Father. And he does this in the power of the Holy Spirit, who, as the Bible testifies, is no other than God himself. God is the Triune God who reveals himself as the Father in self-veiling and holiness, as the Son in self-unveiling and mercy, and as the Holy Spirit

[1] *C.D.*, IV, 2, p. xi.

in self-impartation and love. In this way the content of revelation is definitely given in the doctrine of the Trinity. In addition, as became clear in the course of the *Church Dogmatics*, Barth upheld a penal substitutionary view of the Atonement. Sin has been expiated because Jesus Christ suffered in our place the accusation, condemnation and punishment which is due to us from God. This is the victory of grace over human enmity against grace.

In all this Barth's theology represents a rediscovery of the value of traditional theological reflections—particularly those of the Fathers, the Reformers, and seventeenth-century Lutheran and Reformed Scholastics, not using uncritically, but adapting them to a new theological construction. Barth himself admitted[1] that 'for all the critical freedom that I have had to exercise in this respect, I have always found myself content with the broad lines of Christian tradition'. In attempting a reconsideration of tradition, in particular, in reaffirming Chalcedonian Christology and the Doctrine of the Trinity, Barth has done Christian theology a lasting service. But his own assessment has won only limited assent.

(c) One of the most remarkable aspects of Barth's Dogmatics is his reinterpretation of predestination to make it conform to his theology of his triumph of grace. Mankind is elected to salvation in Jesus Christ, but Jesus Christ is also the only rejected man because God has elected himself for rejection, but man for blessedness. Logically, this would imply the doctrine of universal salvation, but Barth's doctrine of sin is that it has no existence of its own. It belongs to the realm of 'nothingness' and is an 'impossible possibility'. Though it has no ontological standing: its actuality, as in the Crucifixion, can be unspeakably horrible.

For the versatility of his theological construction, and for the massiveness of his heaping up of authorities, future students of theology will turn to Barth's *Church Dogmatics* as a vast storehouse for exploration. But essentially the

[1] *C.D.*, IV, 2, p. xi.

justification for the gigantic character of the *Dogmatics*
would have been if it had been the only possible starting-
point for any contemporary theology. But here Barth has
not proved generally convincing.

Up to the end of the Second World War the influence of
Karl Barth was dominant, but then this gave way to that of
Rudolf Bultmann. Bultmann has been primarily a New
Testament scholar—the greatest of his generation. None the
less, and partly precisely because of the negative aspect of his
rigorous historical Biblical inquiries he has had a profound
and continuing influence on theological study. He has con-
sistently stood with Barth in repudiating the older liberal
theology and in emphasizing anew the delivering grace of
God: within this common standpoint he has diverged from
Barth in emphasizing liberal methods of historical criticism
and in turning to a demythologized existentialism which to
Barth is uncertain in its grasp of Christian truth.

It was his essay *New Testament and Mythology*, published
in 1941[1] which precipitated an active and continuing controversy. On the basis of Luther's understanding of justification by faith, he combined sceptical historical learning
with an emphasis on man's existential needs. He called for
an existential commitment to God's eschatological act in
Christ known in preaching.

Bultmann's theological position, developed in four volumes
of Essays, may be summed up in three main points:

(*a*) 'He took completely for granted God as affirmed in the
theology of Luther.' He spoke of God as 'the sovereign Lord,
who demands death and brings life, who claims our whole
existence for his will, who sets us free to love'.[2] He expressly
exempted God from the category of mythology, and said that
we know God by 'analogy'; but his right to do so is not clear.
For Bultmann man's awareness of God comes from a built-in

---

[1] E.T. in *Kerygma and Myth*, H. W. Bartsch (ed.), S.P.C.K., 1953.
[2] *How does God speak through the Bible?* in *Existence and Faith*, Collins,
1964, p. 201.

prior understanding that is criticized and clarified by the revelation in Jesus Christ.

(b) His whole position was based on a combination of an insistence on the objectivity of scientific knowledge and an almost complete disjunction from it of the personal-existential life of man. Objective history can testify that Jesus lived and that he was crucified but our understanding of the meaning of this fact as God's eschatological event for our salvation, which comes from preaching, has only a tangential relation to the meagre ascertained historical information we know about him.

(c) In essence what Bultmann said in his essay *New Testament and Mythology* is that the New Testament is full of mythological conceptions which are unacceptable to minds reared in a scientific culture. They must be demythologized so that the New Testament understanding of human existence can speak to modern man. Bultmann said that the assumption with which the theologian has to reckon is 'the view of the world which has been moulded by modern science and the modern conception of human nature as a self-subsistent unity immune from the interference of super-natural powers' (p. 7). This seems inconsistent with his saying 'the real purpose of myth is to speak of a transcendent power which controls the world and man, but that purpose is impeded and obscured by the terms in which it is expressed' (p. 11). Bultmann has insisted that 'the importance of the New Testament lies not in its imagery but in the understanding of existence which it enshrines' (p. 11). This understanding of existence faith claims to be true. Bultmann turned to the early existentialist teaching of Martin Heidegger (b. 1889) with its conception of authentic existence as open to the future, as a secularized illustration of the New Testament understanding of human life, which is the true life for contemporary man.

Bultmann held that in the New Testament there is a unique combination of history and myth. 'The New Testament claims that this Jesus of history, whose father and mother were well known to his contemporaries (John 6:42)

is at the same time the pre-existent Son of God, and side by
side with the historical event of the Crucifixion, it sets the
definitely non-historical event of the Resurrection' (p. 34).
Faith in the Resurrection, which comes through preaching,
is the same thing as faith in the saving efficacy of the Cross
(p. 41). In this sense Bultmann's theology is also a theology
of the Word, and not based on history.

The completely dogmatic tone of Bultmann's theology
should be noted. At no point does he seem to consider that
his thesis may be partly true and partly false, or that if it is
necessary to go so far in rejecting what the New Testament
says, this may implicitly involve a rejection of the New
Testament understanding of human existence. His dichotomy
between inward and outward must pose the question whether
he has affirmed a satisfactory basis for believing in God. His
thesis that 'theology is anthropology' is sound if it leads
theologians to see that when we speak about eternal reality
we do so as human beings, and from a human perspective.
We have no direct insight into the nature of transcendental
reality from within. But if this is pressed too far it will
destroy theology altogether.

Since October 1953, when Ernst Käsemann read a paper on
'The Problem of the Historical Jesus' to a gathering of old
Marburg students, Bultmann's ablest students, much to his
regret, have explored the continuity between the earthly Jesus
and the exalted Christ, insisted that much of the Apostolic
preaching is already contained essentially in the words and
deeds of Jesus. By continued historical investigation they
have sought to show critically in different ways the characteristic features of Jesus' teaching and person. A good example
is to be found in Günther Bornkamm: *Jesus of Nazareth*.[1]
This movement is an important positive development.

Paul Tillich was different in his general situation from
Barth and Bultmann in two respects. He took part in a
movement of 'religious socialism' which he saw as a political
alternative to Hitler and had to leave Germany on that

[1] E.T., Hodder and Stoughton, 1960.

account. He was then forty-seven and his general position had been determined, but its working out took place in the environment of America. He became an American citizen in 1940. His legacy is primarily the three volumes of his *Systematic Theology*.[1]

There are in Tillich's theology six main points:

(*a*) Tillich expressed in his theology a unique combination of three elements: (i) *Existentialism*: every man shares in ultimate concern whether or not he directs it worthily. It is to that ultimate concern that Christianity speaks. (ii) *Ontology*: man's ultimate concern is set within a structure of Being. Tillich owed much here to the German idealist philosopher, Friedrich Wilhelm Joseph von Schelling (1775–1854). (iii) *Biblical religion*: Jesus as the Christ expresses the healing power of Being itself, and those who participate in him participate in the power of the New Being by which the existential estrangement of man is overcome.

Essential to this combination is the conviction that theology must find a middle way between naturalism and supranaturalism. Tillich believed that he had solved the problem by resolving natural theology into the analysis of human experience, and supranatural theology to the answers given to the questions implied in existence.

(*b*) *Theonomy* was Tillich's key-word: it is autonomous reason united with its own depth, and that depth is rooted in the Ground of Being, which is Being itself.[2] Tillich rejected both the autonomy of the secular man who shuts his eyes to the religious dimension of life, and the heteronomy of unintelligent submission to external authority. He asserted that God is not another being but Being itself, within which we have our own being. So submission to God is not submission to an external authority but the finding of our true autonomy.

(*c*) In contrast to both Barth and Bultmann, Tillich wove a positive attitude to religion as such into the very essence of

[1] Nisbet, 1950, 1957, 1963.   [2] *S.T.*, I, pp. 94, 227.

his theology. He separated himself from any theology which rejects all religions other than its own, and also from secular non-religion.[1] He found three elements in religion—the experience of the holy within the finite, which is the sacramental basis of all religions; a critical movement against the demonization of the sacramental; and a prophetic movement against the denial of justice in the name of holiness. He described the unity of these three elements as 'the religion of the concrete spirit' but he could not identify it with any actual religion—not even Christianity—and believed that its fulfilment is eschatological: its end is expectation which goes beyond time to eternity.

(d) In the third volume of his *Systematic Theology* (p. 5) he wrote: 'Since the split between a faith unacceptable to culture, and a culture unacceptable to faith, was not possible for me, the only alternative was to interpret the symbols of faith through expressions of our own culture.' And this is clearly what he has done. He insisted that man cannot be man without actualizing his freedom, but that at the same time in the very process of self-actualization, he estranges himself from his original unity with being—a state of dreaming innocence. This conception is more Greek than Biblical, but it did enable Tillich to investigate the condition of estrangement everywhere—notably in art, sociology and psychoanalysis—and to seek for manifestations of Being itself that heal the estrangement.

(e) The answer Tillich found in the manifestation of the New Being in the Biblical picture of Jesus as the Christ. This he asserted to be fact, in spite of his insistence on historical uncertainty about the details of the life of Jesus. 'The concrete biblical material', he said, 'is not guaranteed by faith in respect of empirical factuality; but it is guaranteed as an adequate expression of the transforming power of the New Being in Jesus as the Christ.'[2] There is a threefold emphasis in the Biblical picture—it shows the finiteness of Jesus, the

---

[1] See his book: *The Future of Religions*, Harper and Row, 1966, pp. 86–94.
[2] *S.T.*, II, p. 132.

reality of his temptations, and his repudiation of them in so far as they affected his relation to God and his Messianic vocation (p. 146). He is the bearer of the New Being in the totality of his being, beyond the expressions of it in his words, his suffering, and his 'inner life' (p. 139). He, Jesus, has 'conquered existential estrangement in himself and in everyone who participates in him' (p. 144). 'The peculiar character of the healing through the New Being in Jesus the Christ' is not 'that there is no saving power apart from him, but that he is the ultimate criterion of every healing and saving process' (p. 194).

(f) Tillich's theory of religious truth was essentially a symbolic one. The only non-symbolic statement is the statement that God is being-itself. A true symbol, he asserted, participates in the power of the divine, and through symbolism language penetrates beyond the division between subject and object to a new sublimity of life.

The questions to be asked about Tillich's theology are: is his attempt to bridge the gap between faith and culture satisfactory to either? He stakes everything on his concept of God as Being—not a being. Christian theology must certainly think of God in a unique category and as the Lord of all being, but can it afford to dispense with God as a personal centre who confronts us as well as works within us? Does his insulation of the Biblical picture of Jesus from the historical details do justice to the importance of history for Christian faith?

6. *Christianity and Other Religions*

Here the problem has been to combine an emphasis on the uniqueness of Christ with a humble and fruitful understanding of other religions wrought out in persistent dialogue with them. In this the three conferences of the International Missionary Council—at Edinburgh 1910, at Jerusalem in 1928 and at Tambaram, Madras, in 1938—played an important part in the first half of the century. The Edinburgh Conference saw Christ as the fulfilment of other religions; the Jerusalem Conference stressed the co-operation of all higher religions in combating secularism; but the Tambaram Conference stressed the gulf between the Gospel to which Christianity testifies and its own record as a religion and anything to be found in other religions.

This was due to the impact of *The Christian Message in a non-Christian World*[1] by Hendrik Kraemer (1890–1968). Kraemer's position, reiterated twenty years later in *Why Christianity of all religions?*[2] is that 'Jesus Christ is *the* Revelation of God'. All religions are 'religions of self-redemption, self-justification, and self-sanctification', and so erroneous. But he does not deny that in this errancy there are 'precisely because it is a fleeing from *God*, demonstrable traces of God's activity'. Kraemer's theology was never wholly accepted. This is clear in the notable discussion in *The Authority of the Faith*[3] between a number of theologians who had been at Tambaram. In particular A. G. Hogg drew a distinction between non-Christian *faith*—a life hid in God, immature but not false—and the non-Christian *faiths*—social complexes impregnated with conceptions alien to the Christian Revelation. But Kraemer's argument, though not fully accepted, and contrary to his own intention, broke off discussion between Christian theologians and other religions till the sixties.

But there has come a new emphasis on the need for dialogue, in a changed social situation. A notable contributor has been Ninian Smart (b. 1927) who in an essay in *Soundings*[4] raised the question of truth-tests in religion that might be accepted universally; and in *The Yogi and the Devotee*[5] repudiated the attempted discrediting of religion as such (pp. 99–108) and tried to work out 'a natural theology of religious experience' (Chapters II, III). He admitted the necessity of a 'revealed theology' in Christianity (p. 95), but

[1] Edinburgh House Press, 1938.
[2] Lutterworth Press, 1962, pp. 94–5.
[3] Oxford University Press, 1939.
[4] A. R. Vidler (ed.), Cambridge University Press, 1962.
[5] Allen and Unwin, 1968.

has not yet worked out the relation between this revealed theology and his natural theology. The current task of Christian theology appears to be how to combine an emphasis on *The Finality of Christ* reaffirmed by Lesslie Newbigin (b. 1909)[1] with Smart's natural theology of religious experience or some development or modification of it. We must expect that new insight into this task will come primarily from theologians in 'Younger Churches' situated in centres of predominantly non-Christian culture.

7. *The Theological Ferment of the 1960s*

Whatever may be the later judgment on the 1960s, to live through them involved experiencing a new climate of theological opinion. It should be remembered that Vatican II —in this chapter treated separately—belongs to this ferment, and that it and its effects have both influenced the ferment and been influenced by it. Factors in causing it have been not only an increasing awareness of man's technical mastery of many aspects of his environment, but a sense that the Christian Church had passed out of the Constantinian establishment period of its history into a phase which has analogies with the pre-Constantinian period. In the actual work of theological construction one factor is the exploitation of negative possibilities developed out of the theologies of Barth, Bultmann and Tillich.

The central problem of the decade has been the relation between Christianity and culture. Christianity obviously established deep roots in past phases of human culture. Indeed, the theology it is using was worked out in those earlier cultural settings. But we live in a new phase of culture. How may we in full awareness of it express Christian theology in such a way that it carries conviction? Does intellectual integrity involve a radical reshaping of Christian doctrine including the jettisoning of the idea of God or at least its transformation, or can the affirmation of a transcendent God, confidence in the reality of worship, and

[1] S.C.M., 1969.

conviction of truth in Christian metaphysics be maintained,
whatever reshaping of institutions are necessary?

Within the decade, the debate has been inconclusive. Some
illustrations may be given.

(a) *The Symbolic Importance of Honest to God*

This little book,[1] of which more than a million copies have
been sold, clearly corresponded to a widespread mood. It is
not remarkable for any clarity of thinking or for a profound
awareness of the history of Christian theology. It shows an
astonishing confidence in 'ultimate reality' (p. 29), at a time
when uncertainty as to whether there is anything ultimate is
dominant, together with real uncertainty about what God is.

In assessing the influences upon him that had brought him
to the point of writing the book, Robinson found that three
authors in particular had 'rung his bell': Paul Tillich with his
rejection of supranaturalism, Rudolf Bultmann with his
translation of mythology into a new idiom, and Dietrich
Bonhoeffer (1906–45), who was concerned to work out a non-
religious secular interpretation of Christ for today.

Bonhoeffer—theologian, church leader, martyr—has not
been mentioned earlier, as his influence belongs here. The
stimulating quality of his life and thought for the sixties is
unquestionable. His ultimate theological stature is at the
moment uncertain. He was a disciplined pious Lutheran who
responded deeply to concrete situations in thought and
action. In his posthumous *Letters and Paper from Prison*[2] he
gave expression to fragmentary thoughts about a new type
of Christian theology and action. It took God, Christ and
faith for granted, but sought for a 'non-religious' interpretation of Biblical concepts. It asserted a new understanding of
transcendence, in which 'God is the "Beyond" in the midst
of our life' (30th April 1944). He must be recognized at the
centre of life, not when we are at the end of our resources.
He is met in encounter with Jesus 'as one whose only concern

---

[1] *Honest to God*, by John A. T. Robinson (b. 1919), S.C.M., 1963.
[2] E.T., 1959, rev. edn., S.C.M., 1964.

is for others'.[1] Man has 'come of age' and does not need God
for the solving of his problems. 'Before God and with him
we live without God.' 'Only a suffering God can help.' 'This
must be the starting-point for our "worldly" interpretation'
(16th July 1944). But Bonhoeffer's execution prevented him
from making clear the coherence of his new thinking and
from working out its implications in detail. The influence of
Bonhoeffer on Robinson's thought can be seen not least in his
conviction that the holy is the 'depth' of the common, just
as the 'secular' is the world 'cut off and alienated from its
true depth' (p. 87).

Robinson's book evoked a widespread response, partly
because it was capable of different interpretations. On the
one hand, it expressed a passionate conviction of the truth
and importance of Christian faith; on the other hand it
repudiated the traditional understanding of the term God.
He rejected the idea that God is 'spiritually and meta-
physically out there' (p. 13), and affirmed (p. 53) that 'to
assert that *God* is love is to believe that in love one comes
into touch with the most fundamental reality in the universe,
that Being itself ultimately has this character'.

In his more constructive book *Exploration into God*[2]
Robinson has not substantially altered his thought. Belief
in God as a divine person is simply a transposition of 'the
conviction that reality is reliable—in the kind of way in
which a person can be trusted' (p. 135); but he does not show
that this is plausible. His thinking may be compared with
that of Matthew Arnold (1822–88) who sought to heal the
breach between Christianity and culture in something of the
same way and is open to the same objection of trying to
maintain the religion without the theology. But the problem
of a satisfying Christian theology for today remains.

(b) *Attempts to Construct a 'Relevant' Theology*

(i) *The 'Death of God' Movement.* The 'death of God'
movement is an attempt to come to terms with the fact that

---

[1] *Op. cit.*, 'Outline for a Book'.   [2] S.C.M., 1967.

today belief in God is no longer a universally held belief. William Hamilton is one who has shown in his writings a transition from a 'soft' to a 'hard' radicalism—i.e. from thinking that God has 'disappeared' or is 'eclipsed', or is 'hidden', to thinking that he is irretrievably gone. Now he has lost God, faith and the Church, but dares to call men to the worldly arena 'where men are in need, and where Jesus is to be found and served'.[1] The Christian is to be defined as a 'man bound to Jesus, obedient to him and obedient as he was obedient'. He recognizes that this godless Christology raises the problem of why Jesus should be chosen as the object of obedience, and answers: 'There is something there, in his words, his life, his way with others, his death that I do not find elsewhere.' He insists that this choice is not arbitrary because it is freely made. And out of this godless Christology he gains a new optimism that 'substantive changes in the lives of men can and will be made'.[2]

His associate Thomas J. J. Altizer is a fascinating writer to read. In his book *The Gospel of Christian Atheism*[3] he based his thought on his own interpretation of William Blake, G. W. F. Hegel and Friedrich Nietzsche, and insisted that God annihilated himself in Jesus Christ. He invites us to repudiate all previous theology and trust in his own interpretation of the presence of Christ in the present moment. 'Once we confess that Christ is fully present in the moment before us, then we can truly love the world, and can embrace even its pain and darkness as an epiphany of the body of Christ' (p. 156). He has followed this by a substantial study of Blake as 'the first Christian atheist, the first visionary who chose the kenotic or self-emptying path of immersing himself in the profane reality of experience as the way to the God who is all in all in Jesus'.[4] The danger seems to lie in wait for this

---

[1] *Radical Theology and the Death of God*, with Thomas J. J. Altizer, 1966; Penguin, 1968, pp. 98–100, 52.

[2] See *Frontline Theology*, Dean Peerman (ed.), S.C.M., 1967, pp. 73–5.

[3] Collins, 1967.

[4] *The New Apocalypse: The Radical Christian Vision of William Blake*, Michigan State University Press, 1967, p. xi.

movement of dissolving the substance of Christian theology into simply a passionate concern for human well-being.

(ii) *'Secular' Christianity.* The term 'secular' is a word that has contemporary approval, and has different connotations for different thinkers. It seems often to mean what is taken to be intellectually sound in the contemporary world.

Paul van Buren's *The Secular Meaning of the Gospel*[1] used Chalcedonian Christology and linguistic philosophy to affirm the importance of Jesus as a man 'singularly free for other men', 'whose freedom became contagious' (p. 157). God is now only a word for what we take to be the 'key to the meaning of life' (p. 147). He admits that his interpretation is a reduction of Christian faith to its historical and ethical dimensions, but claims that this leaves out nothing essential. This claim stands or falls with his intepretation of Easter. Easter faith, he says, was 'a new perspective arising out of a situation of discernment focused on the history of Jesus' (p. 132). At Easter the disciples came to share the freedom that Jesus had, to be for others. He acknowledges that the language that he uses is not that of Paul but says that this does not preclude the possibility that our meaning or Paul's may be the same (p. 199). This possibility depends on the assumption that God as a living reality never has been a reality for any one.

Harvey Cox, whose book *The Secular City*[2] appeared in 1966 is a less rigorous thinker. His book is a qualified panegyric on the secular city as the fulfilment of the Biblical understanding of God's purpose in creation. For many people it is a liberation from burdensome restrictions and an entry into exciting new possibilities of choice (p. 40). This is hardly a balanced assessment nor does it provide a standard for judging the humaneness of a city. He says that we speak to secular man of God by speaking of 'man as he is seen in the Biblical perspective' (p. 256). Yet God is 'not simply a different way of talking about man' (p. 259), and he meets us 'in the events of social change' (p. 261). Cox's intention to

[1] S.C.M., 1963.   [2] S.C.M.

relate the God to whom the Bible witnesses to twentieth-century city-dwelling man is plainer than his achievement.

Ronald Gregor Smith (1913–69) has a very different approach. His *Secular Christianity*[1] is a Bultmannian study of 'faith in the context of history, history as qualified by the reality of Christ as *the* eschatological event, and secularity as the real possibility offered by the reality of Christ' (p. 8). God is known only in history and encounter with him there yields a faith open to the future. Apart from his initial assumption, Gregor Smith's book is a moving exposition of generally accepted Christian truth, and demands a depth of religious insight that is far removed from anything specifically secular, and there seems no reason why it should specially appeal to contemporary man.

(iii) *Empirical Theology.* A thinker who like Paul van Buren has responded to the insight of analytical theology in curbing metaphysical pretentiousness is Ian T. Ramsey (b. 1915); but he has used what he has learnt in a very different way. Starting from the publication of *Religious Language—An Empirical placing of theological phrases*[2] in 1957 he has developed in a number of publications the theme that we have experience of certain situations which provoke discernment and invite commitment. In his *Christian Discourse: Some Logical Explorations*,[3] he has spoken of the different way in which cosmic disclosures were understood in Greek and Hebrew tradition (p. 21); insisted that 'doctrinal discourse about the Atonement is worth nothing if it is not unambiguously related to the disclosure of God in Christ at the Crucifixion' (p. 60); and throughout asserted that we can be sure of God, who is disclosed in cosmic disclosures, but that our theology must be tentative (p. 89). This is an insistence on the truth of what is discerned in Christian faith, combined with a persistent attempt to translate the formulation of it into logically more satisfying forms. It remains to be seen how far this method of writing theology will be generally accepted.

[1] Collins, 1966.   [2] S.C.M.   [3] O.U.P., 1965.

(iv) *A Theology of Hope.* Jürgen Moltmann's book *Theology of Hope*[1] represents a theology with a secular concern which boldly stakes everything on God's raising Jesus from the dead (p. 165). Communion with the risen Christ is set out as the way for man to become man, and his still hidden future can be sought in Christ (p. 196). 'As a result of this hope in God's future the present world becomes open for loving, ministering self-expenditure in the interests of a humanizing of conditions and in the interests of the realization of justice in the light of the coming justice of God' (p. 338).

(c) *Is the Process of the Universe a Key to the Understanding of God? Process Theology*

An approach of a very different kind is that of the Process-theologians, who have taken up again the thinking of the mathematician-philosopher A. N. Whitehead (1861–1947) and developed it. This movement owes much to the philosopher Charles Hartshorne (b. 1897), who has expounded a dipolar panentheism in which the universe belongs to the 'actuality' of God but not to his 'essence', thus elucidating the meaning of God as a living God actively responsive to the universe of his creation. The process-theologians affirm the dynamic nature of the universe achieving integration by the mutual expression of love. The love of God is grounded in the process, though its climatic expression is to be found in Jesus Christ.[2] The responsiveness of God to his creation has been stressed since the seventeenth century, so that some elements in this theology are not new. It has links with the thought of Teilhard de Chardin. It remains to be seen whether or not theologians think that it comes too easily to the conclusion that God is love.

(d) *The Word of God and Tradition*

A wide-ranging study has taken place in the 1960s exploring the relations between Scripture and Tradition, which

---

[1] 1965; E.T., 1967.
[2] See *Process Thought and Christian Faith* by Norman Pittenger, Nisbet, 1968.

have been shown to be much more complex than was understood in an earlier period. Scripture is itself part of tradition
and tradition arises both out of what is present and also out
of what is absent from tradition. The study of the way in
which the different communions have dealt with this problem
is a fascinating one. One notable product of the discussion
is *The Word of God and Tradition* by Gerhard Ebeling.[1]
This whole discussion is part of a new discussion of the
question: What authority ought the Bible have for Christians
today?[2]

(e) *What Conception of the Person of Christ Can We Now Hold?*

In contrast to the preceding decades, the sixties mainly
explored ways of conceiving the presence of God in Jesus
other than that given by the Chalcedonian model. Three
instances may be given.

One is that of Maurice Wiles (b. 1923) who, in his essay
'The un-assumed is the unhealed'[3] has used his patristic
learning in arguing that there are no grounds for affirming
that the relation of divine to human in Christ must have
been of a different order from that to which man is to be
brought.

A second is that of John Knox (b. 1900) who in *The
Humanity and Divinity of Christ*[4] insisted that there are only
three possibilities in Christology—adoptionism, kenoticism
and docetism. It is essential to the Gospel that Jesus was a
human being in the same sense as other men. Knox did not
locate the Incarnation specifically in Jesus but in Jesus-in-
the-midst-of-his-own, in other words in the nascent Church.
His conclusion was that 'the divine Lord is no other than the
human Jesus exalted—his *divinity* thus being a transformed,
a redeemed and redemptive *humanity*' (p. 113). This raises

[1] Collins, 1968.
[2] See James Barr, 'The Authority of the Bible. A Study Outline'; in *The Ecumenical Review*, Vol. XXI, No. 2, April 1969, pp. 135–66.
[3] *Religious Studies*, C.U.P., Vol. IV, October 1968, pp. 47–56.
[4] C.U.P., 1967.

the question: is Incarnation in the traditional sense a living intellectual option?

A third instance is that of Wolfhart Pannenberg (b. 1928). Pannenberg's fundamental position is that Jesus is the final revelation of God since we know, because of the Resurrection, that he is the first instalment of God's final Kingdom. Pannenberg has insisted that theology cannot base itself on arbitrary decision or assertion but must respond to what has happened in history and placed the revelation of God in Jesus in the widest setting of the history of the world. In his Christology[1] he propounded a 'Christology from below', with an incisive criticism of the two-nature doctrine (Chapter 8), asserting that the true affirmation is 'this man Jesus is God'. Though we only know it through the resurrection, Jesus in his historical dedication to the Father is identical with the other aspect of his existence—the Eternal Son in relation to the eternal Father (p. 337). This conflicts with Knox's approach and the debate continues.

(f) What Conception of the Atonement Can We Now Hold be True?

F. W. Dillistone (b. 1903) in The Christian Understanding of Atonement[2] surveyed the history of theology in this field, against the background of man's alienation, in terms of four ranges of comparison—cosmic, social, family and individual —and within each range of comparison of two types—one an analogue of corporate experience and the other an example of individual achievement. He was particularly incisive in rejecting the traditional association of the death of Christ with ideas of punishment and substitutionary penalities (Chapter 5 and p. 215), though Pannenberg (Chapter 7) accepted this as the true meaning. Dillistone looked for contemporary examples of the four ranges of comparison and in each type, by which to commend the Atonement today, but except in individual experience is not successful in finding them. This evidently is a field to be explored.

[1] E.T., *Jesus God and Man*, S.C.M., 1968.   [2] Nisbet, 1968.

(g) *Is Not the Patristic–Reformation Tradition the Only Basis that Does Justice to the Objectivity of God, in this Being in Positive Alignment with Contemporary Science?*

The contemporary theological ferment has not induced T. F. Torrance (b. 1913) either to question the reality of God or to take seriously religions other than the Christian. Instead he has reaffirmed the outlook of Karl Barth in a wide-ranging series of historical and constructive essays *Theology in Reconstruction*,[1] and a sustained exposition of *Theological Science*.[2] We must start with the given object and conform our minds to it, and for theology the given object is the concrete act of God in Jesus Christ. Here God has not only objectified himself for man but has provided from within man, full, adequate and perfect reception of that truth. The last three hundred years have been 'a great struggle between the objective Word of God and the master-ful usurpation of the human reason', but also theology has been driven steadily back upon its proper object.[3] Torrance holds that it is scientifically false to begin with epistemology (p. 10). Where there will be disagreement is whether 'the given', with which theology starts, is what Torrance says it is.

The discussion of the 1960s has clearly not solved its essential question. No solution can be satisfactory which does not affirm both the real existence of God, and also the real importance of man's responsibility in secular life. Christian theology needs for its well-being not only more penetrating insight and clarification but also the empowering that will come from a widespread new confidence in the vitality and relevance of Christian truth.

Retrospect

If now we look back on these nearly four hundred years of Christian theology, how shall we estimate them? If we judge them by absolute dogmatic standards drawn from some period in the past, whether Patristic, Medieval or Reforma-

[1] S.C.M., 1965.   [2] Oxford University Press, 1969.
[3] *Theological Science*, pp. 7, 50, 84.

tion, or by fidelity to the Scriptures of the Old and New Testaments treated as absolutely inerrant and not subject to assessment of their truth or historic reality, they may well be seen as a period of retrogression. But if they are seen as a sustained and continuing attempt to find the right way of expressing the truth that is in the Christian Gospel in a time of rapid and extensive social and intellectual change, we may well think that in spite of many flaws and blemishes they deserve our respect and gratitude.

The task of Christian theology is to articulate Christian truth clearly in a way that is appropriate to its environment. The dangers are plainly those of undue accommodation to elements in the environment, and false rigidity and archaism in the formulation of essential Christian truth. One remarkable feature of the endeavour throughout the whole period is the concern of Christian theologians to apply the most searching standards of truth to their own discipline. If Christian theology cannot stand up to the test of truth it is worthless. And the test has been applied rigorously from within even more than from without.

The task of Christian theology in the future will be at least as dangerous and as difficult as ever it has been. One thing is certain. It will not be able to dispense with the freedom from ecclesiastical domination of the eighteenth century, though it must keep sensitive to the faith and life of the Church. It must not attempt to stand outside the search for a true historical perspective of the nineteenth century. It must come to terms with the sense of the twentieth century, that in a new technical world civilization, in which man has great mastery over many aspects of his environment, and in which the Christian tradition has to exhibit its truth and relevance in the context of many religious traditions and attitudes, there is required a new idiom of Christian theology which brings to light in a new way the life-giving truth of the Christian Gospel. To that extent, whatever the outcome, there can be no going back.

INDEX